£4—

On loan to Babette
from NWMC 1-3-80.

Summer's End

Summer's End

BY
ARCHIE HILL

SHEPHEARD-WALWYN
LONDON

ISBN 0 85683 024 0

Printed in Great Britain by
Western Printing Services Ltd, Bristol
and bound at the Pitman Press, Bath

SHEPHEARD-WALWYN (Publishers) Ltd
4 Perrins Lane, London NW3

When summer's end is nighing
And skies at evening cloud,
I muse on change and fortune
   And all the feats I vowed
   When I was young and proud.

From hill and cloud and heaven
The hues of evening died;
Night welled through lane and hollow
   And hushed the countryside,
   But I had youth and pride.

The year might age, and cloudy
The lessening day might close,
But air of other summers
   Breathed from beyond the snows,
   And I had hope of those.

They came and were and are not
And come no more anew;
And all the years and seasons
   That ever can ensue
   Must now be worse and few.

So here's an end of roaming
On eves when autumn nighs:
The ear too fondly listens
   For summer's parting sighs,
   And then the heart replies.

A. E. HOUSMAN

Prologue

My great-great-great-grandfather knew the Black Country valley of the West Midlands when it was forest-fleeced and rich with field's harvests, before the Industrial Revolution came and disembowelled it and hung its hide up to dry. His was the last generation to see it so, where no change had come since the Romans. He was born into a Green Country where deer still bred and roamed; and when he died it was a Black Country where only machines and a forest of too much misery thrived.

After twenty years of absence from my birth-place, I wanted to go back. As increasing middle-age stared back at me every morning from the shaving mirror, so did boyhood, beckoning. Some poet once wrote that every man should return to his birthplace at intervals, to breathe his native air. And insidiously, for years gone, the Black Country had been pulling at me like a mother-magnet. So when Derek Smith, a television producer with BBC Birmingham sought me out, I didn't need much encouragement to pack a suitcase and 'go home'. And, indeed, there was a great deal of personal pride inside me that my writings about the Black Country had prompted Derek to reach out for me, to make a television series called 'Archie Hill Comes Home'. It was like receiving an award for services rendered, a medal, or perhaps a scholarship.

We spent several weeks making the series of films and sometimes, to find the *real* Black Country, we had to dig a bit on the deep side. But we dug well and found little bits and pieces tucked away, little roots and tendrils of it.

Probably men of my generation are the last of the fully Black Country race, the last echo of it. We can span back through our fathers' memories and grandfathers' memories, and when we are dead there's an end to it. Our sons and daughters will have entered into the New World completely, where roots and traditions have little meaning. They've gone to broader horizons—broader but not, I think, as valuable. A quality of life has gone away. I don't mean that the younger people are shallow, or that the old Black Country men were saints. I don't mean that at all. I just mean that something has gone away, never to return; something that was the life-blood of a locality and of an era, and of a people.

Perhaps the most surprising thing that happened to me personally whilst we were filming was the realisation that, as a child brought up during the Great Depression, I had experienced some golden chapters of childhood; that not all of my memories were dark and bleak.

During the creating of the series, we filmed in iron foundries, along canal sides, in dreary dismal streets, among towering office blocks and modern shopping-centres, in glass-works and brick-yards, in fields where dogs were raced, and in pubs. We met people, young and old, rich in craftsmanship and memories. Time after time I almost saw myself as a boy standing on Black Country street corners, watching the world go by; saw myself as a lad down the cut-sides, or walking the patch-work fields which lived between the foundries and the growls of industry.

'If you were asked to put six articles in a box to be sealed for posterity' Derek asked me one day 'to depict the Black Country and its people, what would you put in?'

I thought about it deeply, then gave him what I'd written:

'A Blue Brick, for its strength and durability.

An iron nail, because that's how it all started.

A "nope", a bullfinch, because that wild-bird is the old Black Countryman's favourite. Tough, chunky, cheeky and aggressive.

A reed taken from a canal.

A phial of sweat, mixed with beer.

And a piece of crystal cut-glass to show the beauty which existed in men's minds and the gentle skills which existed in their hands, in utter contradiction and contrast to the strength which lay there also.'

'Going home' was strange and nostalgic. I had thought my re-stirred memories would all be on the sombre side, coloured by the pre-war Depression; but, strangely, I recalled many happy memories of people and places gone away for ever, which couldn't be recorded on film, only re-shone on the mind itself in colours rich and clear and permanent. I recalled and relived one particular school holiday when I was eleven or twelve years of age. . . .

1

I COULD hear the milk-cart in the street. The horse, Bugger,
stamped his feet irritably every time it had to stop. I knew the
horse was called Bugger because that's what the milkman
called him.

'Hey, you Bugger. Give over ... Hold on a bit, Bugger ...
Whoa, you Bugger.'

I lay in bed and could hear Bugger's iron-clad feet clipping
the tarmac like four giant ice-skates. Sometimes he snorted
and the sound came to me like wind blowing in a chim-
ney. The sounds of the milk-urns were thin as tinsel for the
empty ones and solid-thick for the full ones. I lay abed, sharing
with two brothers, and wouldn't open my eyes. I tried to
make my ears tell me things. I made them pierce the bedroom
walls and stand in the street to let me know if it was raining
outside. They couldn't hear any sounds of rain but I mistrusted
them. It *had* to rain today because I didn't want it to. I tried to
make my ears read the sky for sounds of clouds, rain-clouds,
bumping into each other like bullies in a playground. I tried to
make my ears listen for the sizzling sound of sunlight, like
bacon frizzling in a pan. My ears were liars because they told
me nothing, and that's the biggest lie anybody or anything can
tell. The lie of silence; which doesn't exist.

I didn't open my eyes. I stretched them. Stretched my eye-
lids. The dark purple of tight-shut eyes gave way to warmer
red. I held that colour and tried to examine it. Streaks of lighter

4

colours painted across my lids, flower-colours. I stretched them
a bit more and there was golden yellow, the colour of pollen
sticking to a bumble-bee's belly. I took a deep breath and opened
my eyes. Sunlight snatched them towards the bedroom window, and the dazzle of blue sky brought me fully awake. I
climbed out of bed and went to the window and it was a fête-
day of summer warmth and sunlight. It pleased me the same
as pop does when it tingles bubbles at the back of your nose. It
was a glorious day and not a threat of wet-clouds anywhere. The
narrow street was dusty with sunlight, so rich that even the
dark shadows it couldn't reach took some heed of the sun-glow
and mellowed into warm mahogany.

Bugger, the milk-horse, was letting the shafts of the cart hold
him up while he swished flies away from his back-end with
sweeps of his tail. He looked bored to death. He wouldn't be
happy until the round was done and the leathers and chains
taken from him, the huge collar hung on its peg in the stable,
and he himself turned into the fenced freedom of his paddock.
Two or three of our women were clustered round the cart with
their platter jugs. The milkman was standing in the cart,
plunging his long dipper into one of the tall urns and then
pouring the snow-whiteness into the jugs. As they went away
up their entries to their back-kitchens the milkman took a stub
of pencil from behind his ear, wetted it with the tip of
his tongue, and wrote their owings into his tally-book. The
women would settle with him come Saturday dinner-time,
when their men got paid. The window sashes creaked and
complained bitterly as I pushed the bottom window up and
stuck my head out.

'Good morning, Bugger,' I shouted down. The milkman
looked up at me.

'I'll bugger you, if I get my hands on you,' he said, 'you
cheeky young sod.'

I got dressed and raced downstairs, swilled my face at the
cold water tap in the brew-house, hunted around for some hair-
oil. A long time ago I'd had a tin of brilliantine given to me, all
thick as cart-grease and blue as oil. It smelled like a ton of

flowers pressed into the space of an oxo-cube. I liked to put it on my hair thick as thick, so that every strand of hair was matted into the next, so that the whole of my head looked as if a brown shining helmet was sitting there. Trouble was in school once, me sitting near the window and the sun pouring in, it had melted and run all down my face and neck in little nice-smelling rivers that weren't very nice after all. Sticky little rivers all over. 'I always suspected it, Hill,' Teach had called across the class-room, voice acid-deep, 'that what few brains you'd got would melt. Go to the cloakroom and wash them down the sink.'

I had to win about six fist-fights at play-time to stop kids calling me 'sink-brains'.

My brilliantine tin was empty but I wouldn't chuck it away. There was a handsome man smiling a paint-smile from the lid, and he was really a photograph of the man I was going to be when I grew up. Him and me both had shared the magic of grease-thick oil-blue brilliantine and it had got into our bones and would stay there forever. But in the meantime my horse's mane of hair wouldn't stay put without some sort of dressing, so I put a blob of margarine on the palm of one hand, rubbed it with the other until it melted into thinness, and scruffed it into my hair. It smelled strangely . . . stank was nearer the truth. It smelled like dog-dirt.

We had no boot polish in our house so I rubbed the toes of my boots with a crust of bread to draw some lingering vestige of oil to the surface of the leather, then wiped them over with a piece of rag. Inside the crotch of my trousers was a patch that showed if I splayed my legs apart but if I kept my knees fairly close together nobody would heed it. I'd got a girl's blouse on, nice-clean, and the buttons had been put to the other side so's I could bluff it out if anybody *did* say it was a girl's.

I went out the back-kitchen door, down the entry and into the street. The sun was painting it dust-white. I stopped near the wall which kept the yellow river Stour from piddling onto our doorsteps, and looked into the skin-works. The stink of it was gagging. Sharp as acid. I could see hot men working in there; like snowmen they were, all covered in white dust and crusted salt as they cured the skins. The high-up windows of the factory let searchlight paths of sunlight carve through the glooms. I felt malicious as rumour, looking down at the workmen. I'd got a full day's freedom in front of me and they'd got a term of imprisonment. The factory had only bits and pieces of glass left in the windows. The workmen had smashed them to let a bit of fresh air and coolness come in, since the windows themselves had probably been stuck and jammed since Charles Dickens. Come winter cold, the men would stick rags and newspaper into the holes to keep the stink-warmth inside with them. My belly felt warm in knowing that they could only look wistful at the sunlight while I could walk in it. I waited at the wall for five minutes until the man I was looking for came out into the work-yard pushing a skiff.

'Joe,' I shouted, 'can I have me apple now instead of tonight 'cos I'm going on a school trip and I won't be back in time.'

He rested against the push-arms of the skiff. Loaded up with salt it was, and him covered in the dust of it. Reminded me of Tom Mix in a picture, where Tom Mix crossed this desert and was all white and covered. Only Tom Mix had got his horse Tony and not a squeaky-smelly-groaning trolley.

'Wheer bist yo' off to, then?' Joe asked me, like he was my dad.

'On a school trip.'

'Wheer to on a school trip?'

'Stewpony.'

'Thet's no bloody trip. Yo've only got to fall out'n bed and yo' bist theer already.'

'We'm going on a canal boat. All my class is.'

'Ar, then.'

'So can I have me apple now?'

'Who sez ah'n got an apple?'

'Yo've got a tree full at home.'

'Ar, then.'

'So can I have it?'

'Ar, then.'

7

He fished into his jacket pocket, came out with a rosy apple. He wiped it on his jacket sleeve, held it up to the light like a man holding up his ale glass.

'Ketch,' he said, and threw it up to me. I caught it.

'Thanks, Joe,' I said.

'Ah'd as lief come with yo' as stop here working,' he grunted, bending to the skiff. 'Have a good time, young 'un.'

I trotted over the foot-bridge which spanned the railway line, across Turner's field. The blackberry bushes were in final flower, with green fruit-studs thrusting through the flowers. Cowslips dotted everywhere. There were cows and sheep in the top fields, but in the dips were small derricks standing stern over holes in the ground. Coal pits. Only little 'uns, but men worked down there inside the holes. There were clay pits as well, and at the back of these was a brick-yard. It was a sprawl of mud and ooze, with stacks and banks of bricks stuck together like hedges. The fire-ovens were in the middle of the yard and women worked there, handling the bricks and stacking them as they came out of the cooled-off ovens, or hauling them off in barrows to stack them further out. Big women they were. Catch a belter off one of them up the ear-'ole and you thought you'd been kicked by a bloody shire-hoss. I could see one woman standing inside the cooling-down oven and she'd got nothing on except a pair of clogs, a man's cap and a pair of bloomers that looked like two tents side by side. Her titties flapped about as she worked.

I left the fields behind and crossed the high street, then round the back-doubles to school. Most of my class were already in the playground. They looked all different to an ordinary day. Some of 'em were lucky and had got best shirts and trousers and shoes and dresses on. Not many of these. Most of us wore what we wore every day, but mayhap our faces were better scrubbed and our hair slicked back with brilliantine, margarine, or tap water and spit. I found my mate Noggie Garrett and because he didn't see me coming up back of him I thumped him at the side of his neck with my fist.

'Silly sod,' he grumbled, 'what was that for?'

'Because,' I answered. I took the apple-core out of my pocket, brushed and rubbed the fluff from it.

'I saved you the core,' I said.

The pain in his neck disappeared like magic.

Four of our teachers came into the playground and one of them blew a whistle. We lined up immediately, like soldiers on parade. Two of the teachers came down each rank of us, one carrying a satchel and the other a large cardboard box. The teacher with the satchel placed two pennies into all of our sticky hands. Two-pence for spenders. That meant eight gob-stoppers at a farthing each, or four ha'penny ice-cream cornets. The gob-stoppers were best because with care and not too much mouth spit, one could be made to last an hour. There was an art in the sucking. Gob-stoppers were made up of layer upon layer of different colours, and you'd got to keep rotating the giant sweet in your mouth so that one colour melted away completely and not in patches. A great deal of comradeship could exist between two mates and a farthing gob-stopper. One lad would suck through from one colour to the next, take it from his mouth and wipe it, then pass it to his mate who'd suck through to the next colour.

The Teach with the cardboard box stopped in front of each kid and gave him or her a paper bag. Inside the bag were two buns with sugar on top, two bloater-paste sandwiches, and an apple. They wouldn't give us free oranges because they reckoned we'd get the juice down our fronts, and eat the peel as well. With our two-pences clutched in one hand and paper bags of fittle in the next, we were marched from the playground and into the street. Noggie walked like an Indian Scout, on the balls of his feet and with his shoulders scrunched forwards, and with his eyes ominously screwed up to search the horizon for enemy. His mouth was as tight-lipped as his buck-teeth would allow. A wench with pigtails admired him. I gradually got to walking on the balls of my feet with my shoulders hunched forwards, mouth grim, and eyes like battle-slits.

'Silly bugger,' Miss Pigtails said to me, 'why'nt you walk proper, then?'

'Belly button,' I said fiercely, 'backside and bum.'

'Please Miss,' she shrilled, outraged, 'he's swearing at me.'

Teacher's stride never faltered and nor did she look at me; she just put out a meaty arm like a swimmer breast-stroking and clipped my ear a good lowking that made it ring like Christmas bells. Noggie lost his Red Indian stalk and grinned with delight.

We went through the back alleys that led to the High Road, crossed at the traffic lights, through some more alley ways and finally we came to the cut towpath. The teachers made us walk in single file so's nobody could push anybody else into the water. The dirt-walk of the towpath was deep-engraved with the marks of horses' hooves, big as dinner-plates. Moorhens scattered from the reeds as our tramping feet startled them, and they raced fan-shapes of water to get to the other side. Whirlybird dragon-flies stitched more colour on the wind than a dozen gob-stoppers shared by two dozen mouths. Miss Pigtails trod in a pile of horse shit and sank into it up to her ankle socks and she started to cry.

'It's nice wi' custard,' Noggie told her, 'yo' wants to try it some time.'

We came to the boat-wharf and our narrow-boat was waiting for us. Sixty feet long she was, cleaned and scrubbed as a new 'un. All round her sides were lorry-tyres, painted white, but with pick-outs of paint in the shape of flowers and leaves. The hold of the boat was latticed with wooden benches for us to sit on. The gaffer of the boat was already at the tiller, puffing a clay pipe. He looked a sight to warm a snowdrift. He'd got moleskin trousis on, wi' leather belts under the knees. He'd got a checked shirt, squared off in reds and yellows and edges of white, and a scarf round his neck that would have done proud to any wench walking out on a Sunday morning. Round his waist was a leather belt two inches wide, with a brass buckle that was prob'ly pirate's gold. A black bowler jaunted from his head. His mustache was part mustard-coloured, a sure sign that he was a snuff-sniffer like my grandad was.

He'd got a Stafford bull-terrier dog alongside him, and the

dog looked a bit like his gaffer. The boat was low in the water, and a wide gang-plank led in to her. The teachers lined us up and told us to go on board quietly and carefully. Miss Pigtails 'oohed' and 'ahhed' as if she were climbing the rigging of the wrecked Titanic and the water was two miles or someat under her. She blarted away there like an old crone at a christening.

'Ah can see her knickers,' Noggie said loudly, 'they'm white wi' a yellow patch on the arse.'

Miss Pigtails went aboard abruptly with no more to-do about her. She glared at Noggie, and he gave her his Indian look.

'Saft thing,' she said, 'you didn't see my knickers. They'm not white, for starters.'

'Yo' mustn't be wearing any, then,' Noggie told her, 'What ah sid was yo're bum and the yellow bit was a bruise.'

A horse was led from the wharf stables and taken forwards of the narrow-boat. He was hooked up to the tow-rope. Eighteen hands, big as an elephant, gentle as a deer. The kids had started to sway side to side, impatient to be underway. The boat sucked and lapped at its mooring like a thirsty mouth.

'Do' rock the bloody boat,' the Steersman grumbled. 'You'll have me in the waeter else, and ah cor't swim.' But the smile in his eyes belied the grumble in his mouth. He shed the mooring rope and clucked to his horse. We moved away, slowly, into mid-stream. A great cheer ripped from our throats and the horse startled a bit and broke into a trot. Then settled back to a slow easy pace which made the water bubble gently at the prow of the boat, like a babby crooning in a crib.

'It's the life,' Noggie said, 'be Strewth it is ... ah'm going to pass all me exams and be a boatman when ah leaves school.'

'So bist I,' I answered, 'if we can get through grammar-school we stand a fair chance of being one.'

'It takes guts,' Noggie said, 'if the boat gets sunk and yo'm master, yo' has to goo down wi' it.'

'Silly bugger,' I said, 'only navy captains go down wi' their ships.'

'And cut-boat masters,' Noggie said seriously, 'they has to

sign a paper saying they'll goo down wi' their boat if it gets sunk on the cut. They takes an oath to do it.'

We looked into the murky depths of the cut, trying to see the sharks and giant octopuses waiting on the bottom. We looked back at the Steersman there at the rudder with new respect, feeling as if we should stand up and salute him.

The two of us, Noggie and me, were nearest the Steersman. When we'd got used to him and him us, we started to talk with him. He made boat steering look easy.

'Come up by,' he said to us, 'up here with thee and I's'll teach you the ropes.'

No second invitation was required. We squeezed across the catwalk which flanked the cabin and got up there with him. One of the teachers looked as if she were going to tell us to stay put where we were, but the Steersman winked at her cheeky as a young-blood with a wench lined up, as she blushed a bit and left us be.

'Put yo're hands on the ram's head,' the Steersman said to us, 'and feel how I'n got it.' The ram's head was part of the tiller, and by putting our hands to it we got the 'feel' of boat-steering.

'It's easy,' Noggie said after a bit.

The Steersman pointed the stem of his pipe at him.

'Everything's easy, me lover,' he said, 'after yo'n made it so. It's the building up to it that ain't so bloody easy. A thing's easy when yo' does it wi'out thinking about it. Tek hold.' He let Noggie take full control, leaving me green with envy on the inside. Noggie started to lose control. The boat's prow pointed bankwards and rode in as if it were going to ram. The Steersman put out a strong quiet hand and corrected the angle.

'Ar, it's easy,' he said softly, 'to them as know's what they bist about.'

Down in the hold the kids were singing, with a Teach waving her hands like she was conducting. Kid's stuff. Noggie and me were in the back-end doing man's stuff. Noggie swapped his Red Indian look and donned a sea captain's. He stared at the water ahead, eyes slitted against the wind and spray. He stood with legs wide apart, riding the roll of the sea. One hand was hooked by a thumb into the waistband of his trousers, within easy reach of his pistol. His eyes scanned the roaring seas ahead, looking for the top-sails of a pirate vessel or the periscope of an enemy submarine, or puffs of smoke from the guns of a Spanish fort. At one time he got confused about time and place and stood there with an imaginary whip which he cracked and broke against the backs of the kids there in the hold, making them row faster and faster. The Roman galley cleaved the cut-water from Stourbridge to Stewpony, whilst Ancient Britons cowered in the flanking woods and dingles, covered in woad and confusion.

'Wouldn't an engine-boat be better?' I asked the Steersman, 'better than hosses?'

'Hosses have got dignity,' he answered, face lined and weather-brown, 'and engines bist messy noisy and stinky. Ah started with hosses and ah'll end up with hosses.'

'When did you start with hosses, then?'

'How old bist yo'? Eleven, twelve? Ar, then—ah started afore I was as old as yo'. Eight years, ah was, when ah worked a boat for the fust time. Wi' my dad. Him steerer and me boat-boy. Then by time ah was sixteen ah'd got me own butty-boat.'

'What's butty-boat, then?'

'The one that's towed behind another. When ah was eighteen ah took over me own master-boat.'

'Engines bist best,' I said. 'They'm stronger. They can pull more.' He tamped thick twist-tobacco into his clay bowl, stuck the stem in his mouth and sucked the smoke in. The pipe had only got a short stem. The bowl nearly touched his nose.

'It's broke,' I said, 'you're pipe's broken.'

'Ah broke it mesen.'

'On purpose?'

'Ar.'

'Why?'

'Because when it's proper long, it got in front of me eyes. Ah could see it. Wi' it broken off, ah cor't see it. Don't get in the way, this way.' I could hear spit bubbling and cooking inside his pipe.

'Twarn't so long back,' he said, 'hundred and twenty years or so, mayhap a bit more . . . burdens and loads were carried by hosses and mules. Pack horse trains, they was called. All over. They carried coal and iron and all sorts o' stuff in panniers strapped to their backs. Now yo' listen to me—one hoss or mule could carry no more than a hundredweight, 'cos the going round abouts was that rough. But when the canals got cut, it was found that one hoss could pull sixty tons wi' little effort. You see, me lover, cuts bist flat. There's no up hill and down hill on waeter.'

'I like engines,' I said, 'they don't need stabling and they don't need resting. They goo on forever.'

'Ar, and pisons the waeter on the way. Pisons the fish and the moorhens. Buggers the swans up by slicking oil on their feathers. A hoss does none o' that. Waeter's free and natural, and a hoss is close friend to freedom and naturality.'

We came up on a wide sweep of bend.

'Tricky, this,' he said, 'trickier with a hoss-pulled boat than an engine one. Wi' an engine, yo' can back up by reversing if yo' finds yo'm gooing in too sharp. Cor't reverse with a hoss. Yo'n got to plan every move afore yo' comes into the bend—goo in too tight and yo'll hit the bank wi' yo're front. Go in too loose and yo'll find yo're arse-end slapping t'other bank. Too much slack in the rope and yo'll drift all over. Too tight, and yo'll like as not mek it like an elastic band that'll pull the hoss into the waeter.'

We cleared the bend in one flow, smooth as cream off the top of a milk bottle.

'We'm coming up on locks, soon,' he said, 'and when we bist through we'll be eight feet lower. Like ah said, no uphill and downhill on cuts. The locks smooth the bibbles out.'

I admired him.

'Yo' knows a lot,' I said.

'Ar,' he answered, 'a bloody sight more than yo' does, and nor ah've ever bin to school.'

14

The lock did indeed smooth the bibbles out. The Steersman unhitched the horse and walked him down the incline from the lock-gates to the lower water level. He clove-hitched the tow-rope to a hitch-rail specially placed for that purpose, leaving enough freedom for the horse to crop grass from the verge. The lock-master came out of his little house and put a huge key, like a tractor starting handle, into position. He turned the key slowly and below him, in dark glooms and depths, sluice gates opened and let the water boom and bellow. The water level between the two gates started to rise, frothing and bubbling as it came up to the same level that we were on. When it had reached our level it quietened and soothed itself, with just a few bubbles still guggling and complaining. The gates near us were opened fully and we passed into the lock, pushed in by the Steersman and the lock-master. Then the gates and sluices were closed tight at the back of us and the front sluices opened. Out roared the water into the lower level, belching and thundering and kicking up a fine spray and mayhem of wetness. The kids in the hold stopped singing and huddled together as the boat sank lower and lower, flanked by high brick walls which threatened to topple inwards, the walls all slimy and wet and dripping from water departed.

'Women and teachers first,' Noggie shouted hoarsely, 'and I'll shoot the first land-lubber who tries to take to the boats.' I sprawled easily at the tiller, forgetting to keep my knees to-gether so's the crotch-patch didn't show. Miss Pigtails eyed me nervously, but I soothed her with a smile to let her know that I'd got everything under control. I pursed my lips as if they clenched a clay pipe and she scowled and turned away, thinking I was blowing her a kiss. The boat settled at its right level and the second gates were opened up to set us free. The Steersman hitched the horse back on and a shrill cheer went up from the kids as we got back under way. The open countryside flanking us was wide and blazing in sunlight and I didn't want the journey to stop. At the end of it all us kids would clamber out and then walk in regimental-twos to Kinver Edge, which was a sheer bloody waste of time when you stopped to think about it, because who wanted to leave the boat only to sit down in a field to eat sugar-topped buns and lick gob-stoppers. That was kid's stuff, and narrow-boats were man's stuff.

Anyroad, we came to Stewpony and off we had to get, to walk the distance into Kinver. From the top of a hill I looked back at the narrow-boat which would wait for our return. It looked like a painted chip of wood down there, nestling in the water, tiny through distance. The Steersman slipped into the cutside pub even as I watched, the Stafford bull-terrier panting at his heels.

'Ah'd as lief stop with him,' I said to Noggie.

'He's give me something to think on,' Noggie answered, 'and that's me being a boatman when ah grow up. Ah'll be me own gaffer with a hundred boats, and if yo' keeps your apple core for me I might let yo' work for me.' One of the teachers was going on about King Charles, how he'd come by this way on hoss-back ahead of a posse of Cromwell's soldiers, to cut through Stourbridge and Wordsley village. The way she went at it, she sounded like she'd got a crush on Charlie.

'Piddle on him,' Noggie muttered. 'Who's he when he's at whum. Meself, if ah'd-a bin around ah'd've bin on the Roun-heads' side and stuck me bayonet up Charlie's arse. Who wants to bother with him when there's boats to ride.'

I agreed. I put my mind to work. Sod this for a lark, climbing with a bunch of kids over Kinver Edge, listening to teacher's rant on about history, when we could've stayed on the boat and listened to the Steersman. You didn't bloody well *talk* history —you lived it. And how could you live history sitting on your patched-arse by the gorse-bushes eating sugar-cakes? No different to being back in the classroom, with mayhap the roof lifted off to let the sun in.

'Goo and tell our teach ah've got the belly ache,' I told Noggie, 'Goo on, then.'

I sat down clutching my belly and made my eyes tight with pain.

'He's got belly ache, miss,' I could hear Noggie telling one of them.

'*Stomach* ache,' she corrected him, 'he's got stomach ache. Say it.'

'Yes, miss,' Noggie obeyed, 'He's got stomach ache—his belly's playing him up someat awful.'

Teach came back with him.

I groaned up at her.

'It hurts, miss.'

She looked worried.

One of us had better take you back,' she said, 'on the bus.'

I gritted my teeth manfully, keeping my knees together so's she wouldn't see the patch in my trousers' crotch.

'I's'll be alright if ah can lie down a bit,' I said, 'if ah don't have to move much it'll go away. P'raps if ah went back to the boat and lay on one of the seats, miss.'

'Yes,' she said, 'that might be for the best. What have you been cating?'

'Only the sugar-buns,' I moaned, 'that's all. And a green apple.'

'It's the green apple,' she decided, 'Go back to the boat and lic down. I'll tell someone to go with you.' Noggie stepped into the breach, volunteered himself.

'Ah'll stay wi' him, miss,' he said stoutly, 'ah don't mind giving my outing up to stay by him. He's my mate.'

'He should be alright if he stays quiet,' she said doubtfully, 'he's just got a bit of colic. Stay with him, then. If he improves you can both come to Kinver Edge and find us there.' She went back to the other teachers and kids, and they disappeared over the brow of the hill, leaving Noggie and me marooned on a desert island which was surrounded by sharks and the island itself inhabited with tigers, snakes and hostile natives. Noggie and me fought a rearguard action to the creek which used to be a canal and the stockade which used to be a narrow-boat. I got wounded five times but they were only flesh wounds and we'd got this magic stuff wi' us which you couldn't actually see, but once you poured it on, wounds and scars disappeared. We'd used about a gallon of the stuff by the time we got back to the creek and the stockade.

17

The Steersman came from the pub carrying a big jug of ale, and climbed back onto the boat. He was surprised to see us.

'Thought yo'd gone on a picnic,' he said, 'was a bloody quick picnic, that.'

'We got fed up being wi' kids,' I answered, 'we'd liefer be here with yo'.'

'Soever you'm here,' he said, 'yo' can muck in with me. Fancy some cut-oysters? Fresh took from the canal?'

We nodded and he went into his cabin and came out with a flower-painted bucket holding mayhap two dozen oysters. He took a knife as big as a cutlass from his belt, inserted the point between two flush-edges of shell and prised them open like hinged jaws. As the jaws opened they made a plopping noise like grandma kissing your cheek, and then a slow whooshing noise as the air came out. The flesh was creamy-grey and shiny, and the Steersman took it from its bed of mother-of-pearl, slopped it into his mouth and swallowed it. He opened some up for Noggie and me.

'Get 'em down you,' he advised. 'Put hairs on yo're chest, they will—on the *in*side.' We swallowed dutifully.

'Yo'll not fare bad,' he said, 'on a two-or-three dozen of these a week. Food of the Gods, is cut-oysters. 'Specially wi' a coating of pepper on 'em. Strap into 'em, chaps.'

We strapped into 'em. He quaffed from his beer jug, the froth of it foaming his mustache. He belched with satisfaction, stood up, went ashore and back into the pub. He came back with two bottles, chilled from the cold of a pantry sill, and gave one to each of us. 'Get it down thee,' he said, 'that's home-brewed nettle pop. There's aught to crave more on a day this hot, not if you're lads like I once was.'

We sat in the stern drinking the pop, trying to count the bubbles as they rose behind our noses. Delicious it was, herb-flavoured and sharp-sweet. The Steersman disappeared back into his cabin and we could hear him rummaging around in there. When he came topside again he'd got little tins and bottles of paint, and a jam-jar filled with brushes. 'I's'll just finish that cabin panel off while I bist waiting,' he told us. 'I don't reckon on seeing the kids come back for three or four hours. Time enough to fettle the boat up.'

He fettled the boat up. He mixed paints on a piece of wood, making it serve for pallette. We watched him enviously, our mouths lingering on the taste of home-brewed nettle pop but envious of his complete authority, his boat-ownership. One of the cabin panels was blank, just painted flat white and no more. He took up a piece of chalk, reddish in colour, and put magic lines, curves and marks on the panel. Secret marks that spoke their own language to him. Then he took up his paints. Part of his tongue was stuck out from between his lips, in concentration. Noggie's and my tongue came out an equal length in sympathy. He painted a foreground of green meadow with a pool of water coming out at our eyes and reeds and rushes to frame it. The green meadow slowly rose skywards and was crowned by a castle with drawbridge raised, and the turrets stood out from blue sky and white clouds. We watched the magic come out of his mind and into his hands and on to the panel. The detail built up bit by bit, stroke by stroke. Each blade of grass stood out sharp and individual, each ripple in the water belonged to a separate cause. In among the reeds he painted a moorhen and chicks, and even as he painted them they were in quick paddle-flight to get away from his brush. He painted a kingfisher in flight and the colour from his crest and wing tips flashed fire as if the real sun were beating down on them. I watched in amazement as the picture grew, and there was a weep of feeling inside me because I wanted to grow small and step inside the picture and walk that meadow under the blue sky and wave back to Noggie and the Steersman, then take my shoes and socks off and paddle in that water.

'How do you do it, mister?' I asked him, and waited breathlessly for the secret. He scratched his head.

'Ah don't rightly know, me lover,' he answered, reflecting. 'What I think ah does is to make a picture come into me mind. When it's theer, ah meks me mind shine it onto the panel, like ... like a magic lantern, sort of. Then when me mind's put the picture wheer ah wants it, ah just draws round it then fills it in with paint.'

He stroked his brush against a detail.

'Theer's nothing to it, really,' he said. 'If yo' likes doing someat it comes easy in the end. Enjoying the werk meks it come easy.' He finished the panel picture, cleaned his brushes with turps, and put them back into the cabin.

'Ah'll teach yo' how to do it,' he said to me personally, ignoring Noggie, 'any time you've a mind. Ah reckon yo' might have the nack for it.'

Noggie pretended to ignore this favouritism.

'He's no hope at drawing,' he said, 'I bist a betterer drawer than him.'

'Yo'm modest with it, ah will say that,' the Steersman murmured, 'and that's a bloody currency won't get you very far. Here, then, ah'll show yo' 'uns how to mek fish rods.'

'Ah don't care for fishing,' Noggie answered, 'it's an owd man's game, is fishing.'

'Ar, then,' said the Steersman, 'don't let me trespass on your babyhood. Yo' hang on to it while you'n got it. And let me tell yo'—I had my arse kissed by my mam as well as you did, when ah was little. Then when ah got out'n nappies ah couldn't wait to get a fish rod in me hands.'

'I'd like to fish,' I said, 'can ah come to your wharf one day and fish?'

'Any time yo've a mind. And bring yo're mate if he's got a mind as well.'

The day passed too soon and the sun slanted westwards when we heard the kids coming back with the teachers. They crocodiled down the hillside and came back to the boat and I hated their guts for disturbing us.

'You're better, then?' Teach asked suspiciously, seeing me up there with the Steersman and Noggie, as if she and her brood had nought to do wi' us. The Steersman gave a slight grin.

'He's mended,' he said. 'I made him lie down until ten

minutes agone, and he's back in shape. Good enough shape to help me hitch the hoss on, and we'll get underway.'

I went with him to gather the horse in, helped him put the huge collar round its neck and attach the tow-rope. The kids all looked tired sitting there in the hold, but there was no time for tiredness in the likes of me. I'd got to do a man's job of helping to get the boat back to its wharf and take my turn at the tiller. Noggie was just a bloody spare nuisance hanging around. He should be in the hold really, with the other kids, but as long as he kept out'n my way it wouldn't over-matter.

'Gee-up,' I called to the hoss, 'else ah'll light a fire under yo're belly.' Teach glared at me.

'Stomach,' she hissed, 'the word is *stomach*.'

'It says belly in the Bible,' I said back, not cheeky but dead-plain, 'and you read the bit about it in assembly yesterday morning, miss.' I thought Miss Pigtails looked at me admiringly. The Steersman coughed from behind his hand. Then he took a smooth round pebble from a tin and tossed it with a fair sting at the hoss's arse-end. The horse lumbered into a rolling trot.

'That's better,' the Steerman said, 'now we usn't have to light a fire under his belly.'

2

Gʏᴘ Tʏʟᴇʀ was my dad's mate really, but I liked him betterer than I liked my dad and wished he *was* my dad. He was big and tall, not stoop-tall or fat-big. He was straight-tall, over six feet of it, and muscle-big. His belly was flat as a glass-works marvering-slab, and just as tough as the steel it was made from. He'd clench his belly muscles hard and have me punch hell out of it.

'Goo on,' he'd tell me, 'sink yo're fissis into it. If yo' can make me wince, ah'll give you a penny.'

I'd punch hell into his belly until my fists were bruised and sore, and like as not he'd roll a fag while I was doing it and take not a blind bit of notice.

He was a walking book as well. Not just one book, but a bloody library full. Betterer than any of our teachers, he knew more than any of them all put together. In his day he'd been a chain-maker and also a pitman, hauling the coal from underground. In his day? It still was his day because he'd only just turned thirty and wore the years of his prime; but work was a bit thin on the ground everywhere, wi' long dole queues and men standing in 'em like they were queueing up for the hangman in Winson Green prison. Many a gaffer wanted Gyp on his work-team—he was worth two-or-three other men put together—but he'd got a bitterness inside him that told the gaffers to go fuck themselves.

'Ah'm a man,' he said to me when I asked him why he

wouldn't work. 'On my own two legs, ah bist a *man*. Ah'll not work for erra-body who wants to cut my wages when it suits 'em. Ah'll do a fair day's work for a fair day's pay, but ah'll not werk like a bloody donkey and then thank them as meks it so.'

'How'll you get by wi'out work?' I asked him, 'with no money coming in and all?'

He smiled at me, brown eyes warm with laughter.

'Ah'll mek music,' he answered, 'like one or two more round here. Ah shall fiddle what ah wants, and devil tek the hinder-most.'

He was thoughtful for a while.

'Sithee,' he said, 'ah fiddles what ah wants and if ah'm caught they'll call it thieving, up in Brierley Hill court they will. But the gaffers fiddle the werkmen, and it's called thrift and economy. It's called "balancing the nation's books", but all it amounts to is fiddling 'em.' He rolled a cigarette, thin as a matchstick it was with just a few strands of tobacco in it. Two puffs at it and it was gone, leaving nought but ash.

'Yo' ought to roll 'em fatter,' I said, 'they'd last longer.'

He shrugged.

'That's how yo' rolls 'em in prison,' he answered, 'and once yo've got into the habit it's difficult to get out'n it.'

'Was prison bad?'

'It were bad enough. But I reckon it were worse in my feyther's time.'

'Prison run in your family, then?'

He laughed.

'Not so,' he said, 'only the actions that lead into prison—actions brought about by objecting to the system. By trying to put the system to rights. My grand-dad's dad, now tek him—he ended up on a convict ship that took him to Australia and left him theer until he died.'

'What'd he do to earn that, then?'

'He made a secret organisation—we call 'em Trades Unions today. But in his day yo' either got hanged for belonging to one, or deported on a one-way ticket to hard labour. I would've liked

23

to've known my great-grandfeyther. Ah reckon he was a man's man.'

He was silent for a while, tamping on his own thoughts, chewing the cud of personal dark memories.

'Ah went to prison because I thraped a bloke,' he said at last, 'thraped him good. Ah put my fists to him and spoiled his looks.'

'What for, then?'

'Ah come home this time,' he said, 'ah'd bin on the tramp all day looking for work. Ah'd walked far as Birmingham and back, and when ah come whum my mam's in tears by the ash-grid wi' this Means Test feller going at her. We'd got no money, sithee, and the Means Test came to check up on what we'd got, afore they'd give us a ticket to get some groceries. And he upset my mam ... told her to sell her kitchen chairs and things afore he'd put his signature on a note. Her were upset, my mam. So I upset him. I's'll not forget him. He'd got a chocolate voice, yo' knows? Educated sod. And wore plus-fours like as if he were going to play golf. Ah walked in and he spoke to me like I was dog-shit. So ah belted him out'n the back kitchen and into the yard. Then ah spaced a few into him, a few good 'uns. Knocked him all over. Then the police came and took me away and ah did two years. And when ah came out ah was finished wi' the system ah fought in the trenches for.'

He laughed suddenly, wiping the gloom from his face. He rumpled my hair with a hand half the size of a number-nine shovel.

'Forget it, young 'un,' he said, 'there's better days in store for yo'.'

'How can it be,' I answered, 'when all the men bist out of work. Ah suppose me and Noggie 'ull leave school and goo straight on the dole queue.'

'We's'll have a revolution afore then. We's'll put a few of the fat-arses against the wall and shoot 'em by then.'

'We had one of them,' I said, 'Teach told us about it in school. The civil war wi' Cromwell.'

'His bit was only a fart in the wind. We'n got nigh on a

million trained men from the trenches, now. All they want is a leader.' He reflected on that.

'Trouble is,' he said, 'leaders bist thin on the ground. The sort of leader's we'll be needing, that is.'

He pinched the ember from his thin cigarette, put the dog-end into his tobacco tin for re-use later on.

'Only two blokes ever entered Parliament with the best of intentions,' he told me, 'and that was Cromwell to empty it and Guy Fawkes to burn it.'

I walked most places with Gyp. Or rode round 'em on our home-built ramshackle bikes. Gyp had turned up at our house once with a cart-load of bits and pieces, the cart and pony that drew it belonging to a mate of his. Gyp tipped the bits and pieces on to the pavement outside our house: a bike frame, couple of wheels, handlebars.

'Here, yo',' he said to me, 'ah've had yo're interests at heart. Ah've collected all these bits from tips and tacky-banks and if yo've got an ounce of gumption yo'll turn 'em into a bike yo' can ride.'

He left me staring at the rusted up bits of iron and clip-clopped off down the street. I sorted the odds and sods out, then got to work. After two days I'd got a pedaller that would run alright. No brakes, no mudguards. But I could pedal it and it was *mine*. I soon got the hang of making it stop. I just took a foot off the pedal and stuck it against the side of the rag-packed tyre, pressed it there until I came to a halt. If I were going at a fairish lick when I did it, the tyre rubbed friction against my boot so that the boot itself felt hot, like it was stuck inside a baking oven.

Weekends, when school was done, I rode out with Gyp much as I could, and Noggie was jealous of this, because it made him seem only like a spare-time mate of mine. But I didn't want to share Gyp with him. If Noggie tagged along with us, then the boys outnumbered the men, and Gyp would talk down to us, like we were only kids after all. But if I went with him on my own he talked with me on his own level, as if I was an equal and not a tagged-on afterthought. We covered hundreds of

25

miles, mayhap thousands, in our runs out together. He told me the names of the places we passed through and although they'd always existed on my doorstep I'd never really thought, before, to consider their names. He told them to me, repeating them like they were music notes from a mandolin. Brierley Hill, Pens-net, Mouse Sweet, Bumble Hole, Holly Hall, Silver End, Amblecote, Tippity Green . . . as Gyp told me the names I swear I heard forest pixies playing flutes while wood creatures listened. I tried to imagine each place at the time of its christening, when the landscape was lush and green and thick tree-fleeced. Place names which were music-ghosts of another age that had dwindled into a distance beyond the grasp of my imagination.

But the places as I looked at them were mostly pylon-straddled, with here and there cooling towers thrusting up like tumours. Back-to-back housing estates, railway-sidings, giant bleak sprawls of iron foundries and iron-forges, chain shops and brick-yards. Black pit-derricks stencilled against the sky; and ridges of earth spread and sprawled like wrinkles of skin on an old man's face, where the Industrial Revolution had come and disembowelled and left forever wounds.

We'd pedalled to the bottom of Mucklow's Hill on the road to Birmingham, dismounted and pushed our bikes up the long climb. At the very top we set our bikes down and sprawled on a patch of green verge which flanked the road, looked out on the valley which was my home.

'You'n got chance,' Gyp said to me seriously, the visor of his cloth cap pulled low over his eyes to keep the sun out of them, the muffler at his throat loosened to let some coolness get in. 'You'n got the chance to get educated, which is a sight more than I ever got. Drink the education in, chap, and mek someat of yourself when yo' grows up. There's nought down there but iron and sweat or coal and dust.'

'Ah can be an iron-moulder or a pit-man,' I answered, 'but best of all I want to be a boatman. To ride the water-ways.'

A horse and cart was descending Mucklow's Hill. The driver had fitted wedge-brakes under the front of the rear wheels. The wedge-brakes were made of wood and the surfaces which came into the road's contact were covered in a sort of thick rubber stuff to enable them to shrug along the tarmac instead of skidding without resistance. The cartman had swung down from his seat and strode at the horse's head, holding at his bridle to stop him speeding up. It was a long steep hill and the cartmen didn't overlike it. If a horse started to let the cart push at him he'd like as not keep picking up speed until he ended up as a dead sticky crushed mess at the bottom of the hill. More than one had gone that way. Sparks the colour of white lightning sizzled from the horse's hooves. 'Will he mek it?' I asked Gyp nervously.

'He'll be well enough,' Gyp answered. 'The farriers shoe the hosses on this run wi' spiked shoes. Little spikes on the under side of the irons, so's they can grip.'

'Canal horses don't need that kind of contranklement,' I said, 'they'm always pulling a level load. There's no up hill and down hill on waeter.'

'No bloody future in it, neither,' Gyp answered. 'What's in cut-work for the likes of thee? It's an old man's job now, and by the time yo' bist old enough to earn your fittle, cut-boats will be finished with. Gaffers and folks send their stuff by rail and lorry, now. Waeter bist too slow. There'll not be much on it left when yo' grows up.'

'What'll ah do, then?'

'Get from under, that's what. Goo where the clean work is. Goo where yo' don't have to sweat piss for every penny earned. Go to work in a good suit and a clean shirt and collar, and come home the same as yo' went.'

'Office work is for cissies.'

'Ar, then. Wish ah'd bin born a cissy.'

He was silent, looking out and over the dark valley. To the South and West we could see the green sweet ripeness of Worcestershire with its slow roll of hills that marked Clent, and the standing hills of Shropshire with Kinver Edge ridge standing as sentinel to them. We kept our backs to the North because Birmingham was there, like a dark shadow threatening.

'Yo' knows someat?' Gyp said to me, 'when my great-great-grandfeyther stood on this spot wheer we bist sitting he'd see nothing but fields and forests, wi' mayhap a small nail-shop among the tree-clearings. He'd-a looked down theer and would've seen forests as thick as fleece of a sheep.'

'Forests? Here?' I asked, slightly amazed.

'Ar, forests. Thick as thick. All that valley down theer would've been thick wi' woods, wi' patches of clearings put under the plough, and herds of sheep and cows pasturing in the lezzers. The river Stour would've bin clean enough to tek fish from it instead of like it is now, all yellow and pisoned from factories. My great-great-grandfeyther would've stood here and looked down at the heart of a rural England. He would've been the last of the Green Country men in this region.'

I marvelled at it, trying to see the valley covered in forest and with deer timid as shadows there in the tree glooms. But in my mind it was like seeing a painted picture inside a frame; it had no more meaning than that.

'My great-grandfeyther was a first generation Black Country man,' Gyp went on, more to his own thoughts than to me, I think. 'He'd have seen the brunt of change. His eyes would've seen the black soot and thick smoke covering the valley. His eyes would've seen, from this spot, nigh on forty thousand nail-shops theer in that valley. All belching fire and smoke-fug. And his son, my grandfeyther, would have been born into that lot so's he'd've thought it natural enough. He'd no other comparison to steer by, sithee. He'd've thought it all fit and proper enough. Him and my feyther both. But yo', me lover . . . in yo're life time it'll all change over again. Yo're generation will be the last of the full Black Country men. It'll be all finished wi' yo'.'

'Will it be someat to be proud on?' I asked him, 'will it be a sort of honour, to be the last?'

'Some bits of it will, mayhap. Other bits ah'm not too sure on.'

From where we sprawled the Black Country valley beneath us seemed like a toy-village, with here and there a toy railway engine and coal-trucks puffing by. The smoke from the engine stacks waved back against the thrust of forwards motion, the smoke seemed made of something solid that you could go down to and cut with a knife, or chisel, or carve shapes out of with a moulding plane.

'Let's ride on to Cradley,' Gyp said, standing up. 'There's a farrier mate o' mine ah want to call on.'

Gyp's bike had got brakes to it. Mine hadn't. So going down the steep hill towards Cradley he rode alongside me, on the offside, with one hand gripping my shoulder so that his brakes could take care of both on us. His fingers were strong on my shoulder, and it felt like nothing could ever harm anybody with hands like that to protect. I took side-long looks at him, and in my mind I knew he shouldn't be riding an old bike down a Black Country hill; he should be sitting tall and easy in the saddle of a cowboy horse there in the Wild West, wi' a big gun strapped to his hip.

'You should've bin a cowboy, Gyp,' I said aloud. 'You look sort of like a cowboy.'

His teeth were good as they showed through his grin.

'Most of what the American cowboys bist, they took from us,' he said, free-wheeling both of us down the long slope.

'What you mean?'

'We had cowboys here long afore they did.'

'Ah've never seed any cowboys here. 'Cept farm labourers in farms, looking after cows.'

'Less than a hundred years agone,' Gyp told me, 'herds of cattle used to come through these parts on the hoof. Big trail drives of 'em, wi' men on horseback riding herd. Wi' flintlock pistols in their belts or in saddle holsters. Wearing big floppy hats like stetsons. Big horned cattle, brought on the hoof from Scotland. And there was stage-coaches around, things like that. Just like the Wild West yo'm on about. Even the way cowboys of America talk mostly comes from these parts, or at least many of the ways. The Yanks say 'yeah' for 'yes'—and our old English forbears used to say 'yea'. Yanks also say 'sure', as a slang sort of 'yes' ... not so long ago, Englishmen would say 'surely', meaning the same thing. And tek the bloke in America who's called a Sheriff—that comes from the owd English Shire-reeve. Him being the bloke in charge of the law, like a sort of police-man. And posse . . . did yo' know that this country had posses 'way back in the times of the Normans? And yo've heard my muther speak, when her says 'his'n' and 'hers'n'. . . ? American cowboys say the same things—only we used 'em fust, sithee.'

My front wheel wobbled in admiration of him.

'Yo' knows a lot of things, our Gyp.'

He half smiled.

'Ar, ah does that,' he said, 'and most of what ah knows ah keeps to mesen.'

We cycled through cobbled side roads of Cradley, down long avenues of cramped houses which had nothing uncommon, the one with the other. The houses were dirty with smoke and dust. Even the slates on the roofs were in need of a giant's duster. Here and there a woman sat on her front step with her blouse or dress undone, holding a babby in her lap and feeding it titty. Big swollen breasts they'd got and the front of one woman's dress was wet with milk that had missed her babby's mouth. Other kids were playing hopscotch, with the squares marked off on the lumpy pavement with chalk, probably pinched from school. A very young kid, about three years old, was tied to a lamp-post wi' a skipping rope, blarting its eyes out. Some mom had told her older kid to mind the little 'un and it was in the road and naught but a bloody nuisance, and the older one had tied her up with the rope so's she wouldn't wander off. It was no fun for the kid, being tied there like a dog to a kennel.

We rattled along on our bone-shakers, through alleys and over cobbles, swerving our front wheels to miss the piles of horse dung round which the flies droned and buzzed. There was a brewery nearby. We could smell the rich heaviness of malt and hops on the air, a lovely belly-cuddling smell which was halfways betterer than lying out in a field of clover and smelling it.

We went up this entry—a wide entry it was, big enough to get a hoss and cart up—and there was the farrier's yard. We leaned our bikes agin the wall and stood looking at him. Gyp's eyes were smiling in enjoyment of the scene. There was an affection in his eyes which could only be for the farrier busy at his forge. Bathed in the red glow of the forge-fire, like a man standing in the fullness of a summer sunset. He wasn't a young man, the farrier. He was old enough to be my gran-dad. A white bush of hair, close cropped round ears and back of his head, but bushed on top. Like a mass of dandelion-clocks pressed thick-tight together. He was wearing a green denim shirt without a collar, but the collar-stud was stuck inside its hole, glinting in the fire-glow like a piece of gold. His sleeves were rolled tightly above his elbows, high up the biceps, and his arms were nearly as good muscled as Gyp's. He'd got tattoos all over. Snakes intertwined with flowers, and birds and badges, and a pair of hearts connected by an arrow. I thought he'd got a wrist-watch strapped to his left wrist, but when I looked closer I saw that it wasn't a real watch, but tattooed on. Another man stood in the yard, holding a horse by its bridle. The farrier was shaping a shoe on his anvil. He'd got it gripped in a pair of long iron pincers, and the shoe itself was red-hot, and the swinging hammer was knocking sense into it and sparks from it. He held the article up to the light and surveyed it critically. Still gripping it in the pincers, he came from the forge and into the yard.

'Hock him up,' he said to the man with the horse. The man slapped his hand sharp at the back of the horse's offside front leg, behind the knee. As the leg bent, the man drew its hoof upwards. The farrier took it that way, held the bent leg against his leather apron with the underside of the hoof pointed upwards. He placed the red-hot shoe on the hoof-horn, and clouds of blue smoke drifted out like exploding gunpowder. The smell of burning hoof came to my nose, not a nasty smell but a bit like fried pig-crackling. The farrier took the hot shoe away, stared at the burn-pattern made by it.

'Still wants a bit o' trimming,' he muttered. He put the iron shoe back on the anvil, took up a large honing rasp.

'Hock him up,' he said again, and when he'd got the hoof comfortably placed on his apron-covered knees he took the rasp and with quick smooth motion pared off more horn. The horse stood still and perfect.

'That'll do it,' he muttered. He took up the shoe, stuck half-a-dozen long wedge-shaped brads into his mouth, picked up his hammer and hammered the shoe on to the hoof. The points of the brads came out through the sides of the hoof, well below the quick so that there was no pain to the horse. He hammered the points downwards against the hoof-horn. In less than no time he'd shoed the nearside front. Only then did he show that he knew Gyp and me were standing there.

'Now for some fun,' he said to us, 'this bugger don't like having shoes fitted to his arse-end feet. He thinks he's his own gaffer, and nobody's told him that *I'm* his bloody gaffer when it comes to shoeing.'

'Do you want a hand?' Gyp asked.

'I's'll need a bloody block and tackle and a donkey engine on this bugger,' the farrier answered, 'yo' mark my word if ah don't.'

He went back to his forge, hand pumped the leather bellows to make the coke sing with heat and air, then hammered the finishing touches to the two rear-hoove shoes.

'Hold him at the head,' he said to the horse-owner, 'Ah'll hock him up.' He put his hand on the horses haunches, started to slide the hand down its flank to take the hoof.

The horse cow-kicked. A sideways kick which would have lifted the farrier across the yard had it connected. But he was too fly. He side stepped and grinned.

'You bugger,' he said, 'I's'll have you. Yo' might as well settle to it, 'cos I's'll have you.' He balled his fist and sank it strong into the horse's under-belly. The horse retaliated promptly by kicking out with both hind legs. There was enough power in the lunge to knock a house down.

'Put him on the twitch,' he said to the owner. And the man took up what I thought was a riding crop—one of those short leather whip things, with a rope looped-handle to hold. I'd always thought it was a handle, but now I learned the 'handle' was a twitch. The loop was put over the horse's upper lip, and then twisted round and round until it tightened a bit on the savage side, gripping lip and nostrils.

'Keep him tight,' the farrier said, 'and that should hold him while I'm done.' He went round the horse's back end; but the bloody horse kicked just the same, despite it must have hurt his nose and lip to do so. The farrier stepped away exasperated.

'You gone-bugger,' he said, 'yo' think ah was born yesterday? Yo' wanting me to tie you up, tip you over, and shoe you upside down, then? What yo' reckon ah bist, then? A bloody green rookie in the cavalry? Tek his front, Gyp, and us-uns 'ull show the bugger.'

Gyp went to the horse's front offside, grabbed its leg and bent it up. Held it. The farrier went to the nearside back leg and took it up from the ground as easy as picking up a stick. The horse trembled there, afraid because only two feet had direct contact with the floor. It wouldn't move, let alone kick. The farrier shoed it, then both he and Gyp swapped legs and did the other. The job was done.

'Told yo', didn't I,' the farrier said to the horse, 'ah'm the gaffer, not yo'.'

It seemed to me that the horse sulked. Its owner led it clattering down the yard, it stepping gingerly on new iron shoes. The farrier wiped the sweat from his brow with a dirty rag, sat down on the step of his forge, motioning me and Gyp to join him. The two men rolled cigarettes and spoke no word between them until the white tubes were glowing and wisping smoke.

'There's a bottle of cold tay near the anvil,' the farrier said to me, 'if yo' fancies a swallow.' I fetched the bottle of cold tea, drank from it. Sweet and thick and delicious. The two men each took swigs.

'It's almost dinner time,' the farrier said, 'so yo' might as well stop on and share wi' me. Ah'n got some black pudding, cheese and pickles. And a bit of beetroot fresh from my allotment. Drop o' home brewed ale in the keg as well.'

Gyp nodded acceptance.

'Who's this, then?' the farrier asked him, looking at me, 'is he yo're kid brother, then?'

33

'No,' Gyp said, 'he's part me shadow and mostly me mate. Ah'm learning him the ropes.'

'Learning him the ropes,' the farrier grumbled, 'in these days it teks a bit of doing. Strikes me too much time is used up unravelling the bloody knots in the ropes, let alone owt else.' He got up, went inside the forge-house, and rummaged around in there. He came out with a fittle-box, laid it on the step. Went back inside. I heard the ale froth and hiss into the platter jug he held under the keg spigot. He brought the ale on to the step.

'Yo'll have to drink out'n jam jars same as me,' he said to us. 'Ah'n lent me best cut-glass to the Mayor 'cos they'm having a civic piss-up. Here, yo', young 'un—a couple o' swallows o' this stuff's all yo' bist having, else yo'll end up riding that bike o' your'n upside down. Strong stuff, is this.'

He opened the fittle box and took out wedges of home-made bread, thick and nicely yeast-sour. He put lumps of cheese onto the bread, and rings of black pudding, topping the lot with purple slivers of beetroot whose juice soaked into the bread like blood from a bruise. We sat on the step, wolfing it down, and the smell of the food mixed in with the smell of burning coke and burnt horse-parings, and the flat smell of iron. I sipped my ale while the men gulped long swallows from theirs, and the meal was good and wholesome and would have been a treat fit for a king. When we'd finished eating Gyp looked at the farrier.

'Hast done it, then?' he asked. The farrier nodded.

'Ah'll get it,' he said. While he was gone I asked Gyp about the wrist watch the man had got tattooed on his wrist.

'Did'st see the time the tattoo-watch was set at?' Gyp asked me, and I answered that I hadn't noticed.

'The tattoo hands bist set for fower o'clock,' Gyp said, 'and that's the time he gets up every morning, winter or summer, rain or shine. Old Jack theer bist nigh on seventy and he's worked in this forge sin he was nobbut a nipper of seven or eight. Worked wi' his feyther. When he was eighteen, Jack's feyther died. It was then that he had that watch tattooed on his wrist wi' the hands set to fower o'clock. Loved his feyther, he

34

did ... and since his feyther got up fower by the clock every morning to start his day's stent, Jack said he'd do the same. And the tattoo watch was his permanent reminder never to be less a man than his feyther was.'

The farrier came back to us, holding something inside a rag. He gave it to Gyp and Gyp opened it. I caught my breath in wonder at the pistol which Gyp took from the rag. Oh! what a pistol, what a dream of a pistol! Long barrelled and fist-weight heavy to keep it true on target when pointed, the butt plates made from checkered wood to give good holding, the whole of it perfect and pleasing. The farrier took it from Gyp to explain its points. 'It's a two-shot,' he explained, 'sithee? Cap and ball —percussion, they call it. Yo'll load up wi' black powder, and it's easy enough to make yo're own fulminate primers. Yo' can mould yo're own balls out'n lead. Point thirty-six bore, keep 'em a bit on the tight side for fit and that road yo'll not lose any power. Ah've rifled the barrels one and a half turns to give spin and accuracy. Wi' luck and a good eye, yo'll drop rabbits at forty yards.' Gyp took it back and fondled it.

'It's a good 'un, Jack,' he said, 'my oath, but it's a bloody good 'un.'

'If it weren't, yo' wouldn't be holding it,' the farrier answered. 'None of my work leaves my hands unless ah bist satisfied wi' it. But sithee, there's something else. See this?' he took a metal plug from his pocket, a round plug with a thread cut into one end. Gyp looked at it, puzzled.

'There's two of these,' the farrier told him, 'one for each barrel. When you'n not using the gun, yo' threads these plugs into the barrel ends like this, sithee. This allen-key teks 'em out when yo' wants to shoot it. The idea is this—leave the plugs in when you'm not using it, and if the police cop you with it on you, you just show 'em the bunged up barrels and tell 'em its an ornamental piece. Sithee?'

Gyp grinned. 'Jack,' he said, praise rich in his voice, 'yo' bist wasting yo're time putting shoes on hosses. Yo'm a bloody wizard.' He handed the pistol to me to feel and hold, reading the mouth-watering in my eyes.

35

'How much dost I owe thee, Jack?' Gyp asked. 'Ah don't honestly reckon ah can raise enough brass to cover that.' Jack swigged deep from his jam jar of ale.

'Yo' owes me nothing but yo're good will, me lover,' he answered. 'Yo' teks that gun from me as a friend. But ah shaw't say no to the odd rabbit yo' might care to drop my road from time to time.'

'Charcoal, saltpetre and sulphor,' Gyp muttered, looking at the gun, 'ah can get all that from the glass-works and iron-foundries to mek the gun-powder. But ah shall have to buy some fulminate-caps to go on the nipples. Shall get some o' them from Birmingham easy enough.'

'Don't overload the barrel-charges,' Jack advised, 'Ah've tested up to ten-grains. But more than that ah wouldn't like to say—might end up blowing the gun apart, and yo'self with it. Anyroad, put too much powder in and yo'll end up cooking the bleeding rabbits as well as shooting 'em.'

'Did you really make it?' I asked the farrier, 'did you really make the pistol?'

He winked at me.

'Yo'd be surprised what ah can make when ah put's my mind to it, young 'un,' he said. 'There's a bit more to me than being a hosses' cobbler.'

I sighed with envy as I handed the gun back to Gyp.

'When ah'm growed up,' I said, 'ah shall ask you to make me one of them.'

He smiled.

'Ah shall be long dead when yo'm growed up,' he said, 'so you'd best keep on the good side of Gyp here. When he's an owd man and cor't shoot straight, mayhap he'll hand that'n over to you.'

'As long as he only wants to get his hands on a sporting gun,' Gyp said, 'he'll be alright. Just as long as the buggers don't *make* him pick up a long Lee-Enfield, like they did me in the trenches. Shootin' rabbits and game is one thing. Shooting men's another.'

He stood up to go.

36

'Ah thank thee, Jack,' he said to the farrier, 'ah shall treasure it. Ah'm beholden to you.'

'Be done wi' beholden,' the old man answered, 'there's no beholden atween friends. I's'll see you around.'

He went back into the forge-shop and worked the leather bellows to get the fire glowing. It glowed red in the middle and white-hot round the edges, like a red glaring eye fringed all round with over-white eye-lids. The fire-glow threw his shadow on to the wall so that it moved there like a black giant. We watched him for a few moments, him intent upon the work he was doing and shutting us from his mind so that no distractions entered into him.

'See you around,' Gyp called softly, and we pushed our bikes down the rough cobbled entry, and into the street.

3

ALTHOUGH Noggie and me were mates and went to the same school together, I think we were best-mates at the times when we rode out with his dad, who owned a pony and cart. That's how Noggie's dad made his living, with pony and cart. Sometimes he humped things for people, like luggage and bits of furniture, at a fee. Other times he collected scrap-iron which he sold to the weighing-in man up at the Round Oak iron works near Brierley Hill. Noggie was sometimes a bit monty because he'd got a dad with money to always jingle in his pockets, and the inside of their house was fairish with comfort while most of ours were of the make-and-mend brigade. But Noggie's dad wasn't monty—he was a nice man, with many a joke to crack, and a generous hand to dip pocket-wise when we were near a sweet shop or ice-cream cart on a hot day. Sometimes he'd come home from his travels and tell Noggie and me that he'd fixed us up with a bit of pocket-money work for a nearby farmer, according to whatever season it might be. Bit of strawberry picking on a Saturday, or pea-picking. Once, we cursed him from here to hell and back for getting us a Saturday's beet-cutting in a farmer's field back of Wordsley woods. A bitter cold day, cold enough to put icicles dripping from your finger-ends. The frost was in the beet thick and solid, and by the time knocking-off time came most of the frost had left the beet and come into us. The farmer gave us two shillings apiece, and we spent nearly all of it in a jellied-eel and faggots-and-peas shop, stuffing the food into ourselves to work up a bit of personal central heating.

This one day Noggie's dad saw the two of us together in the street, and he stopped his hoss and cart and called us over to him.

'How bist yo' two at carpentry?' he asked us. 'Teks lessons in school, doesn't you?'

We nodded.

'Ah'm betterer than him, though,' Noggie said, nodding towards me. 'He's noggin-headed wi' hammer or chisel.'

'Gerrout'n it,' I replied, 'it's *yo*' who's noggin-headed—that's why yo' bist called "Noggie".'

'He's saft in the head as well,' son told father. 'Ah'm just minding him for his mother. Her has to have a break from him now and then.'

'The pair of you bist so bloody half-witted,' the dad said, 'that if both yo're brains were put together they'd still get the new owner shut up in a lunatic asylum. Hop into the cart, the pair on you.'

We hopped into the cart, the pair of us.

'Ah need a couple-a good chaps at carpentry,' Noggie's dad said over his shoulder, 'a couple of craftsmen.'

'I can make bird-tables,' Noggie told him, 'or dovetailed-drawers, or cornices, or mantel-pieces. I 'spect I could make a staircase if ah'd got the wood. And ah've always fancied making a carved treasure chest—'

'Shut yo're cake-hole,' the dad said, 'what we bist going to do is chop a tree down.'

We digested this bit of information from the back of the cart, waiting in case there was a joke-line to follow. There wasn't. And we could see the ropes and pulley-tackles on the floor of the cart, and the assortment of rip-saws and felling-axes. One thing was for sure—if Noggie's dad said a tree was going to be chopped down, then it was coming down. But Noggie and me looked at each other.

'What's he want wi' a tree?' Noggie whispered, 'is he going to make a bloody clothes prop or someat?'

39

'It's in a field,' Noggie's dad said by way of explanation, without turning round, 'standing all by itself, ripe and prime for felling.' He clucked to his horse and made it move half a pace faster, and it drew us away from the back-to-back forest of houses and into a lane that led to Morgan's farm fields. In the field a solitary oak tree was standing. Noggie's dad reined in, surveyed the tree.

'That's the one,' he said, 'down it comes, cut close to the ground as we can get it.'

He tied the horse by its reins to a gate, well out of range of the tree-fall when it should happen, and him, me, and Noggie hauled all the gear from the cart and took it to the tree.

'Jobb should be here be now,' Noggie's dad grumbled, taking a huge watch from a wescott pocket and looking at its glaring dial. 'Don't tell me we'n come to the wrong tree.' But even as he spoke a familiar figure came across the field towards us. Moleskin trousis with straps under the knees, checked shirt, bowler hat, short clay pipe stuck in mouth. The gay red scarf at his throat blazed brave as a robin's throat against a snow-drift. The Steersman who'd taken our class on the cut-outing, the bloke who promised to show me how to steer a narrow-'un and paint castles and roses on the panels.

'Got a good work team wi' you, I see,' he said to Noggie's dad, 'rounded up all the muscle in the district, looks like.' His eyes smiled as he said it, so Noggie and me took no umbrage. He took a piece of chalk from a pocket, circled it round the tree trunk two feet from ground-level.

'We'll cut it theer,' he said, 'that should do nicely.'

He looked first at Noggie then at me.

'Now think on it,' he told us, 'when we cuts this tree down, wheer will the top of it fall?'

We stood back and looked up at the tree, tried to measure its height with our eyes.

'About theer,' Noggie said at last, pointing to a spot some twenty feet from the trunk of the tree, 'ah'd say about theer.'

'About theer's not good enough,' the Steersman told him, 'if this tree were nearby housens, yo'd have to be more exact than that—otherwise the tree 'ud crash through somebody's roof, young 'un. Yo'd be letting daylight into a few bedrooms. Yo' has to think these things out afore yo' starts on 'em. How tall do you reckon that tree is, then?'

We looked at it again.

'Twenty feet,' I ventured.

'Seventy,' Noggie said, always outbidding me.

'Thirty-five if it's an inch,' the Steersman told us, 'thirty-five feet of good English oak. How'd you measure it exact, then?'

Noggie and me thought about it.

'I could climb it,' I said, 'with a piece of string wi' a weight tied on one end. Lower the string 'til the weight touched ground, then come on down and measure the string.'

'That'd be one way,' the Steersman half approved, 'but it's the long road down, bisn't it. Yo' might fall and break yo're bleeding neck for a start. Now if we had a sextant we could measure it exact. But we hasn't got a sextant, so if we use our native wit and mother nature. Ah told yo' to come at this time o' day for a special reason.' He spoke to Noggie's dad.

'The sun's in exactly the right position for it,' he told him, 'so tek this tape measure and measure my shadow from boot-toe to head-top.'

Noggie's dad did as he was told, and measured the shadow.

'Ah'm exactly five feet ten inches,' the Steersman told the two of us, 'and at this time o' day, my shadow should be exactly the same.'

'What's the measure, then?' he asked Noggie's dad.

'Right enough, it's five-ten,' Noggie's dad answered, 'so ah'll tek the measurement of the tree.'

The shadow of the tree stretched thirty-six feet seven inches. 'See, ah told thee,' the Steersman said. He and Noggie's dad each took up a felling axe, tested the edges with their thumbs. They cut exactly to the chalk mark, one man cutting neat axe-chips from the front and the other cutting from the rear. Soon, looked at sideways on, the tree trunk looked like two huge pencils touching point to point. A full pencil formed by the bulk of the tree and a stub-pencil formed by the two feet or so that was to remain in the ground to rot. The Steersman took up an iron wedge and drove it into his cut with strong blows of a sled-hammer, driving it in so that it almost filled the cut he'd made. The wedge reinforced that side of the tree so that it couldn't swing back on the cut and fall in a direction he didn't plan on. He put down the axe and took up the two-handed cross-saw. Noggie's dad took the other end, and, together they roughed it backwards and forwards across the axe-cut Noggie's dad had made. Noggie and me stood fifty feet back of the tree, just in case. But there was no need. The tree cracked like a pistol-shot and Noggie's dad and the Steersman removed the cross-saw and stepped to one side. The tree trembled there, still upright and showing no full signs of coming down.

'Another tickle with the saw?' Noggie's dad asked him, but the Steersman shook his head.

'The next breeze that fills its head 'ull bring it down,' he answered. And sure enough the next breeze gave it a push and the tree cracked again, then started to slide forwards. It seemed to drop in slow-motion, the mass of branches twigs and leaves at its head cushioning its speed. It came to ground with a solid thump and didn't even bounce, so heavy was its weight. The fallen tree filled its own shadow like iron poured into a mould.

'Right,' said the Steersman, 'now we can all get stuck into it.' We set to and lobbed the branches away from the fallen trunk, leaving the big thick ones to the two men. When we'd finished, the trunk was naked of all but its own bark, and was much smaller now that the twists and head-growths were taken from it. It looked compact and chunky. We set to and lopped the lesser branches from the big ones, then the twigs from these. When we'd finished, there were heaps of graded wood-loppings laid out in neat piles. The lesser twigs and branches we carried down to the hedge and left there, for the farmer to use for repairing gaps. Other stubs of branches we left him for fire-wood. We got all the leaves together for burning at a later day, when they would be dry. The bigger and straighter branches we loaded on to the cart, putting the tools and tackle there as well.

The Steersman packed his clay pipe with thick twist tobacco, looking at the tree trunk critically the while.

'When dost think thee'll drag this over to my place, Wilf?' he asked Noggie's dad, 'thee s'll not carry it on that cart of your'n.'

'Ah'll get it to you next wik,' Noggie's dad said. 'Ah've arranged to borrow a long flat iron cart and an extra hoss. We's'll get it to you, have no fear.'

'It's not far to tek it,' the Steersman said. 'Mayhap yo'll not need to cart it. Put chains on the hosses and yoke 'em to the tree, and let 'em drag it.'

'It'll ride better wi' wheels under it,' Noggie's dad answered, 'just leave it to me. If yo'll not tell me how to drag loads, ah'll not try to tell yo' how to build boats.'

'Fair enough,' the Steersman answered, 'no offence intended.'

'Ar, then,' said Noggie's dad.

We went with the cart the short distance to the Steersman's wharf, and unloaded the branches and logs. Noggie's dad had got another haulage job on and wouldn't even wait for a brew of tea. Noggie hesitated between his dad and me when he realised that I wanted to stay at the boat-wharf. His dad won. I watched him trotting away in the cart, sitting next to his dad. Even as I watched I saw his dad hand Noggie the reins, and I felt a blaze-stab of envy in my guts. The Steersman's wife gave me tea and cakes, and I sat on the house-step sipping and chewing and giving bits of cake to the Stafford bull-terrier.

'What's the tree for, then?' I asked the man, 'the one as we just cut down?'

'It's to mek a boat with. A narrow boat. When the tree is dry and well textured, ah shall saw it into shape for a boat.'

'They bist making narrow-boats out of iron these days. Most boats I see on the cuts are iron-boats.'

'They bist only cargo-boats, for lugging coal and iron and stuff. The boats I meks bist wooden 'uns—there's nought better than wood for mekking a boat you can live in and off. Tek my word on it.'

43

'Ar, then,' I said. Knowing there was no contradiction to what *he'd* said. Laying out in his yard were oakwood planks. Two years ago they'd been standing trees, but the Steersman had felled them and nursed them, peeled them and cut them into planks, rods, laths, beams and struts. Now they were dry and sound-seasoned, with no twists and warps, no inbuilt strains. 'Good timber, that,' the Steersman told me, 'not like yo're bloody furniture timber. All oven-dried, that bist. Standing in a forest last week, and like as not it's a sideboard in somebody's front parlour this 'un. Have to let wood dry natural, otherwise it'll go brittle and have no strength in its grain and fibres. Have to keep turning it this way and that, one end for t'other. Let the sun and weather kiss sensible dryness into it, sithee.'

A skeleton of a boat was standing in a nest of trestles pointing down a slipway which entered the canal. It looked like the bones of a whale standing there, just a skeleton of bones in the shape of wooden pieces.

'She's not very long,' I said, 'that one isn't. She's only about thirty feet. She won't carry much load.'

'She's not for loading,' he said, 'she's for living in. She's for when I retire. Me and the missus will live in her. That's what she's for.' He took up his saws—a huge variety—and held each one up to the light and stared along its length like a soldier sighting a rifle; and if a tooth were out of alignment he immediately attended to it, putting pliers to it and edging it to position. Then he took a file and sharpened the cutting edges of each tooth. When he'd done, he twanged the blade with thumb and forefinger so that the good steel rang with warm music which droned on and on like the sound of a gong. He showed me a tool I'd never even seen before.

'That's an adze,' he told me, 'no different in any way to the one the Good Lord used when he were a lad in a carpenter's shop.'

He opened up his huge carpentry chest, took out the various wood-planes and fondled them. One by one he stripped them, cleaned them, then re-assembled them and laid them carefully onto an old blanket, edgeways so's the blades wouldn't get damaged. The wood grips of every tool seemed to fit his fingers, as if they were tailor-made specially for him.

I worked hard with the Steersman that day. Fetching and carrying, sweeping up the wood shavings that spurted from his planes like bacon slices from a grocer's cutting machine. The Steersman showed me how to select and match the timbers needed for narrow-boat building.

'A boat's got a main central strake for keel, wi' two curves,' he said, 'a strake being a main timber. There has to be one curve at the front and one at the back. Yo' *can* get the curves by steaming 'em in, but that's a bodged job, that is. Puts too much strain on the boat—'sides which, she'd be always squeaking and complaining. Like new shoes, thee knows? Only loud enough to bugger your ears up. Now if we take *this* piece there's one curve already in the grain, mother-nature-perfect and they dosn't come any betterer. That means only *one* curve has to be steamed in, which meks for a better job all round.' Together we worked on the boat standing on its launch trestles. The keel was well laid and well curved at both ends, with not the whisper of a creak in either. I helped fit other main strakes and some of the ribs and lesser struts. Just like the things Teach told us about in school—arteries, veins and capillaries.

'That'll do for today,' the Steersman said at last looking at the reddened sun as it dipped towards its bedtime. 'We's'll have a bite of supper, chap.'

I was reluctant to leave the boat. I thought if we lit paraffin lamps and carbide lights we could work the night through. All I'd got to do was run home and tell me mam and dad where I'd be, and wi' hard work and a few short cuts we'd like as not be able to launch the new boat when the sun came up again.

The Steersman laughed.

'Yo' cor't rush it, chap,' he told me, 'not to do a well-job. Yo' couldn't rush the tree to give us the wood, yo' can't rush the tools to do a good job. Yo' cor't rush yourself and get the best out'n what's in you. Mad-rushing is close brother to laziness, sithee. They'm both upsetting and they'm both worth bugger

45

all.' He carefully put his tools away against the next need of them.

'The boat only needs her skin and flesh now,' he said, 'just needs the inner and outer shell. Once that's done, there's caulking to do—fill the seams wi' strands of oakum, hammer it into the cracks and seams with mallets and wood-wedges. Then cover all over wi' tar and pitch-blende outside and in. Then we'll fit her out. Shackles and linch-pins, post-rings, the like. When her's finally dry ah shall paint her.'

'Wi' pictures? Wi' birds and flowers and castles and roses?'

'Ar. Them as well. Then choose a name for her and paint it both sides of the prow. Hast got a good name for her in thee head?'

I thought about it deep.

'The Viking,' I said at last, 'call her the Viking.'

He considered it.

'Ar, then,' he said at last, 'I like it. That's what she bist, then —the Viking.'

We went inside his house for supper, mugs of cocoa and wedges of cheese and bread. When I'd finished mine he bade me go home before it grew dark, but said for me to come back any time I'd a mind to.

Noggie was sitting on his entry wall, waiting for me in the nearly full-night darkness.

'Yo' were a long time,' he said, 'wha' kept you?'

'I helped build a boat.'

'Silly bugger. Yo' should've come wi' me. We carried some loads on dad's hoss and cart, and I earned a sixpence. Yo'd have got same if yo'd bin with me.'

I felt my heart sink a bit. But then it lifted.

'Meks no odds about a tanner,' I told him. 'What's in a tanner, then? Yo' can spend that in two minutes in a suck-shop. But I enjoyed meself, and the thinking on it 'ull last me longer than half-a-dozen gob-stoppers.'

4

'Why do yo' always come top in art and English, in school?'
Noggie asked me, 'why bist yo' always up front of class, then?'

''Cos I like art and English,' I answered, 'and if yo' likes
doing someat, it comes easy.'

'But you cor't mek a living out'n art and English,' Noggie
insisted, 'no gaffer will pay yo' a wage for them things.'

'It depends,' I said, 'it all depends.'

'Load o' saftness,' Noggie sniffed, 'get yourself nowheer, all
that will.' We were sitting on the top of the tallest hill in the
Clock Fields, with the stockade at our backs and the prairie in
front of us. We had Winchester repeating rifles across our
knees and our keen eyes were sharp as a brace of hawks, scanning the prairie for marauding Indians.

'We's'll have to bury them we'n shot,' Noggie said, pointing
towards piles and heaps of stones up front, 'otherwise they'll
stink and the coyotes will come sniffing round.'

'Let 'em stink,' I answered, 'ah'm not moving on down there
in case it's an ambush.'

'That's good thinking,' Noggie agreed, 'that's using your
head a bit.' He thought some more.

'I see nothing in drawing and reading and writing,' he said,
'not to want to do it all the time. What's writing but words?
What's drawing but pictures, then?'

'It all depends,' I said.

He glared at me with exasperation.

'Depends on what, you silly bugger? You keep on saying "it depends".'

'I dunno what I mean,' I said, 'honestly I don't.'

'It's wenches' stuff,' he grumbled, 'is picture painting and reading and writing. As long as yo' can read and write a letter and reckon up yo're pay-packet of a Sat'day dinner-time, that's all of *that* yo' need do. Yo've got the rest of yo're time to do things.'

'Like what?'

'Well, like playing for instance.'

'Playing's pictures.'

'How'd you mean, you saft bugger?'

'*Playing* paints pictures inside yo're mind. Walking the cuts does. And going in the foundries and glass-works. All them things *paints* pictures...only later on we calls the pictures *memories*. That's what Gyp says, anyroad.'

His Winchester turned back into a stick and he threw it from him.

'Yo'm always wi' the old men,' he criticised, 'nearly all the time.'

'Gyp's not old. Yo're dad's older than he bist.'

'Jack the blacksmith's old. And the boatman. They'm both that old they'll blow away in a stiff wind.'

'They'm not old to me,' I defended, 'they'm my mates. They tell me things.'

'They go on and on and on. Same things ower and ower.'

'You'm jealous,' I said.

'Jealous? What bist ah jealous of, then?'

'Because.'

'Because they don't talk to me as much as to yo'?'

'Jealous because yo' don't understand what they bist telling you.'

'What bist they telling, then? Other than twaddle and bull-shit?'

'Secrets,' I answered, 'they tell secrets. Not hush-hush secrets, they bist other sorts of secrets. Like how things work and why. Like who we bist, who our forbears were—like how-come we'm the Black Country. Like how the Black Country is a place to be proud on and never ashamed.'

'Proud on? Yo'm codding—when ah'm old enough, ah'll not wait to shake the dust of this place from me boots, ah'll tell thee that.'

'Ar, then,' I said.

He glared at me.

'Yo' says ah'm jealous again,' he told me, 'and ah shall challenge yo' to a fight. Saying ah'm jealous is like saying ah bist a coward.'

'It isn't,' I said, 'it's not the same thing at all, it isn't.'

'Ah'm not a liar. It *is* the same.'

'Ar, then.'

'So tek it back.'

'Ah shaw't.'

'I's'll fight thee, then.'

'I'll not fight.'

'Yo'm a coward, then.'

'Ah'm not.'

'Prove it.'

'Ah don't need to prove it. My word's on it. My word to meself.'

'Stand up and I's'll knock you down.'

'Ah'll not stand up. If ah do, and you knock me down, ah shall get up and fight you. I winna fight you. We'm mates.'

Noggie stood up.

'We'm mates no more,' he said,' not 'til yo' says sorry for calling me a coward. Yo'll either say sorry or fight me to clear the air. One or t'other to clear the air. Nothing in between.'

'Ar, then,' I said, watching him walk away.

'Gyp,' I said, 'I got to fight Noggie, and ah'm frit of it.'

He looked deep at me, eyes warm and brown with crinkle-lines of concern on his brow.

'Noggie's yo're mate,' he said.

I nodded.

49

'Well, best o' mates can fall out,' he mused, 'but why bist frit of him. Has he got four fists and a brass jaw that yo' bist frightened on him?'

'He's bigger than me.'

'How much bigger? Ten foot? Twenty foot?'

''bout three inches.'

'Ar, then. So it's three inches yo'm frittened of.'

It suddenly seemed such a small amount I felt ashamed for mentioning it.

'I expect ah shall manage,' I said.

He cupped my chin in one of his hands. I could feel the roughened callouses against my skin.

'No, me lover,' he said, part smiling, 'that's not the road on it. Yo'll be ended afore yo' swings a punch, else. Three inches is piddle down a drain. Let's get it worked out, sithee.' He motioned me to sit on the doorstep alongside him, and he pulled out his battered tobacco-tin and rolled one of his thin prison-style fags.

'To be frittened is nothing to be ashamed on,' he told me, 'as long as yo' knows what it is that's making you afraid. As long as you can *see* what it is. See whatever it is is too big for yo' to manage. F'rinstance, a bloke standing five feet six would be a bloody fool to try'n fight wi' a man standing six foot six. A man wi' a catapult would be a fool to tackle an army tank coming at him. Neither would be cowards because they were frit to death.'

I nodded.

'Three inches is nothing,' I agreed, 'It's nothing to be frittened on.' He didn't heed me.

'Tek a battlefield,' he said, 'wi' guns opening up all round and the shells coming in thick and fast and furious, and men lined up shooting it out wi' each other, thousands upon thousands ... and night and barbed wire and trench-rats and dead men stinking ... it gives you fear, chap. All on it put together nigh on burns yo're mind away. Little bits and pieces of it can make you soil your trousers. This is fear, chap. Fear of what's too big ... there's no sense of cowardice in this type of fear

50

because everything's too big to bear. No matter what yo' does, you know deep down that your little ha'pporth won't show, your little bit of effort won't make a dent anywhere. Dos't understand me?'

'I think so,' I said, letting my mind conjure up a battlefield and me in the centre of it with a snow-white bandage round my brow where I'd taken a bullet-graze, but still up front of my men, hundreds and thousands of them, pistol in one hand and sword in the other, leading my men to the storming of the Hun trenches. And them cheering me like a football crowd. And back of them, safe and sound behind breastworks of sand-bagged-safety, a dozen Generals waited breathlessly for me to signal the victory so's they could rush forwards and pin medals all over me.

'It's false pride to try to be heroic against the odds that can't be budged,' Gyp was saying, 'and no man's got the right of false pride. If he's got it, then he's stupid. He's a threat and a risk to all round him. Self-pride has got value—it's a good currency to carry in yo're mind's pocket. Self-pride comes from knowing what you'm made of, what reliance there is in you, what experience. We'm all brash when we'm young. We'n got no experience when we'm young. We can hardly tell the differ-ence atween cowardice and caution when we'm young, that's the trouble on it. If yo' wants to know what ah feel, then ah wouldn't fight Noggie if ah was yo'. He's your *mate*. If ah was yo', I'd tell him ah was sorry.'

'He'll mont if ah do that. He'll swank over me and think he's bested me.'

'Will *yo*' think that? Inside yo'self?'

'No.'

'Ar, then.'

I thought about it.

'If ah'm not to prove myself,' I said, 'if ah'm not to prove either that ah'm a better bloke than him, or that ah can stand on me own two feet and tek all he can throw at me—and still come back loffing—why'd you tell me all the things yo' does?'

'Like what, chap?'

'Like saying yo'd back down to no man. No matter the odds.'

'I only mean ah'd do that if there was no other way than stand to him. No way at all. When ah'd made up my mind that *that* had to be the way on it.'

'Yo'd back down, then? If yo' could?'

'Ar. I would—if the backing-down had a value to it. Ah wouldn't grovel. Ah wouldn't plead. But ah'd apologise if it would keep the peace, if the person ah was apologising to had the sense to respect my apology.'

'Ah don't understand,' I said, 'yo'm known as the best fighter around. Yo'm always in lots of fights.'

He was a bit uneasy.

'Sithee, lad,' he said, low-voiced, 'ah've not got the education —ah've not got the words to use . . . it's *systems* ah fight, not people. Not really. It's rotten dirty stinking systems. Like my great-grandfeyther did, when they put him on a hulk and sent him to the Australias. I fight agin *systems*. Not as I shall beat 'em—it'll tek millions of the likes o' me to do that . . . and ah'll not see the victory in my life time. *Yo'* might. When ah thraped that Means Test man for upsetting my mam, ah was thrapin' the system. When ah took that head game-keeper on who copped me wi' rabbits, ah was fighting the system which made me fight in the trenches for this land but won't let me share the fruits from it. Sithee?'

A dull light was glowing in my brain, just a slight dull light.

'Ah think ah understand, Gyp,' I answered, 'Ah think ah does.'

'That's it, then,' he said, satisfied, 'You'm getting hold on it.'

'Noggie's not system,' I said.

'Ar, then.'

'Noggie's mate,' I said.

'Ar.'

'So it's not backing down to tell him ah'm sorry.'

'Ar, then.'

'I's'll tell him,' I said, 'tell him ah'm sorry we fell out.'

52

'Do it soon,' Gyp said, 'afore time can get at it and mek it fester.'

I walked with Gyp towards the Frowley brick-yard, the one standing in its own sand-coloured acres, bitter-bleak and mind-worrying. No blade of grass grew inside those acres, no bramble or wild flower, no smile of nature to shed something bright and good into a parched wilderness. I didn't like the brick-yards of the Black Country. They reminded me of pictures I'd seen, pictures which frightened. 'Surrealism' teacher called the pictures. Bleak deliberate landscapes which came out of lonely dreams, or haunt-tinged dreams, the sort that lie only small steps away from nightmares. The brick-yards were like that. Flat, emotionless, littered only with dust and heat and a marrow-sucking dryness. The iron-foundries and glass-works were filled with colours and movements, every passing minute brought with it a different noise and a different picture; but the brick-yards were one long droning picture of sameness and a sort of poverty that niggled inside the mind when it should've been feasting itself.

'Why'd you want to go to the brick-yards?' I asked Gyp, 'there's not much there for us.'

'Want to see a bloke,' he said vaguely, 'who promised me some bricks. Some seconds.'

He saw that I was taking quick steps to keep up with his long ones, and he slowed pace to match mine. I liked it better that way because it meant I was actually in his company, and not like an afterthought tagged onto him. Walking at my pace meant that he'd got full time for me. Gyp was as old as my memory. He was my first conscious memory. I remembered being carried down a hillside splashed with yellow flowers, and over the shoulder of the man who carried me I could see the late-summer evening sky painted into dark and crimson. And against the sky itself, as if cut from black cardboard and stuck on, were looming pit-heads. As the man carried me I could see other men and boys chasing a puff of blue smoke which settled itself and rested until the shouting men drew near, when it lifted on the light wind and soared and danced to further distance. I must have fallen asleep or drowsed in the safe strength of the man carrying me; and even recalling the memory made some bond flow like Light from my secret self to that man who'd carried me. My memory knew the man, only his face was missing ... until recently, when some of my brothers and sisters were teasing their memories to see who could reach back furthest. I mentioned the memory of the man on the hillside.

'Ah remember that,' my dad had said. 'Let's see—ah remember that. Yo' was only a babby at the time—yo' *couldn't* remember *that*.'

'I *do* remember,' I answered.

There was something like awe in my dad's voice.

'It was when we lived in Cannock,' he said, 'when I were a collier in the pits. Yo'd only be eighteen months old, then—how could you remember?'

He considered it, himself peeling back the years which were perhaps rather few to him, but many to me.

'That puff of blue smoke yo'm on about,' he said, 'it wasn't smoke at all. It was Ziah Billing's budgie as got loose from its cage. And Ziah and his mates and all the kids were buggering all over the place trying to catch it. Ah remember that. Ar, I remember it. We'd been up to the Collier's club to listen to Gyp sing, and after we'd done it was him as carried yo' down that hillside.' He was silent in thought.

'Eighteen months old,' he said, 'just fancy yo' remembering that.'

He could sing, could Gyp. When he sang his voice was clear and word-perfect, with not much Black Country accent in it, like as if he owned two voices, one for singing in and one for talking in. When he got excited about anything, or angry, the Black Country showed through even more, guttural and hard as a German I once heard. But when he sang ... things came through pure and clear as mountain sunlight foreign to smoke and the gloom of industry. He was tall and lithe, with brown eyes that had seen much in life and which had come to secret

54

understanding with all that they looked at. But sometimes, when the afterglow of conversation waned and died to its own finished ashes, he'd sit and stare into space, with eyes and face softened to sadness. And I'd take my books and keep to myself until the darkness lifted from him a bit. He'd soldiered in the Great War. I thought war was great, that it gave chance to do brave things and with crowds of people clapping and cheering in the background while you did 'em. Shining buttons and tossing plumes, and more sportsmanship than on our cricket-pitch at school in summer time. Gyp painted different pictures of war with his words, but mostly without words. He painted dark pictures with what his eyes said, and the bitter twist of his mouth. There was no magic in the places of war he spoke of, like there was magic in Crecy and Agincourt our history teacher told us on. Gyp spoke of places called Arras and the Somme, Ypres, and Flanders. The names had a doleful sound, like a bell chiming a single solemn note. Now and then I caught a mental glimpse of Gyp lying out in the mud of Flanders, the cold trenches of the Somme . . . Gyp's dark dim days peopled with too many ghosts.

We stayed at his house one night, my dad and me. Gyp was living at Silver End, a few miles from our place, and the dad and me had walked to see him and left it late for getting back to our own house. So we stayed the night, all three on us sharing the one bed. I got him to tell me, in the comfortable musty dark, about the brave soldiers he'd served with before I'd got born. His voice had an almost weary tinge to it.

'It were a long ago nightmare,' he said, low-voiced, 'where no music sounded.'

He lay quiet in the bedroom darkness, my dad snoring a sleep-full the other side of him.

'Didn't like cold steel, chap,' Gyp said in a quiet puzzled voice, 'the Boche didn't like cold steel. They ran from the bayonets.'

I pounced back, mayhap with a boy's cruelty.

'Did the British like cold steel? Didn't the English run away from the bayonets?'

55

'Couldn't face the bayonets, the Germans couldn't,' Gyp insisted, ignoring my question, 'once the steel went on the rifle, they'd break for it.'

I slept, and woke up to the sound of Gyp's voice shouting and raving and dad trying to word-nurse him from the dream still holding him. Gyp was shouting and bellowing, the sweat pouring from him, the brown eyes I loved so well now bulging and bursting with all the horrors of the world. His mam came in, an old coat covering her nightie, and a lit candle in her hand to see by. She shushed and soothed her son and got him quiet again, and then took me from his bed and into hers so's he'd only got my dad by him. And in her tiny cramped bedroom with its high chest of drawers taking up almost as much room as the brass-fitted bed, she told me not to talk war wi' Gyp anymore. She didn't want him being reminded of things, she said, which made him sob in the long nights. She told me how, afore I'd got born, Gyp had been making his way back through the rear trenches of the battlefield, alone and tired through crumbling deserted communication trenches that men had dug and died to dig. Gyp going back to short leave and short safety ... he'd turned a sharp angle of trench only to come face to face with a German soldier. Quick as the light of destiny Gyp had thrust with his bayonet and toppled life from its citidel. And the German lay in the mud with his blood draining away into ooze and poppies. I knew the way his mother told me that more than any single thing, this one tore Gyp into shreds. Because he learned, after giving the death-blow, that the German lad was unarmed and had crept to the English lines to surrender his body from the terrible carnage all round. ....

Sad, haunting songs Gyp sang. They belonged to a different generation than mine. They came through time lonely and sad and beautiful as a music-box tinkling in a dream of crinolines. They were memories that belonged to older people. *We* came upon them by chance. 'The Last Rose of Summer', 'Mother MacRee', 'Two Little Girls in Red, Sir', 'I Care not for the Stars that Shine', 'Because', 'So Deep is the Night', ... the names never stuck to remembrance, much, but the music always remained. His voice was clear liquid, tenor, and every place where he sang became a landscape of beauty.

'Ah don't like the brick-yards, Gyp,' I told him as we walked, 'they'm mis'rable looking.'

'There's a lot of misery stacked at the back of 'em,' he answered, 'bloody misery that'ud make a concrete-carved Christ weep tears o' blood. My mam was a brick-yard wench, and her mam afore her. As a lad ah sat at my grand-mam's feet in her kitchen. Sat wi' her by the black-leaded grate, staring into the fire in the ash-grid while her talked. Mekking pictures in the fire to fit her words.'

He walked on quiet for so long a time I thought he'd forgot about me.

'The pictures,' I nudged him, 'tell me about the words and the pictures.'

'You'n got a right thirsty little mind,' he said. 'Ar, then. But what's in words and pictures? Oh, my grand-mam talked about the old brick-yards and ah'd listen. Eighteen-fifty she were born. And in eighteen-fifty-seven her started work as a page in the brick-yards . . . the same one as we bist going to now. Her stent started at six in the morning and went on 'til six at night. . . .'

I could see it all inside my mind as he told me. The women and girls coming to work under shivering stars, their clogs rattling over the cobbles and bibbles. Little wenches of seven or eight or nine still nearly asleep on their feet, with mayhap one of the older women here and there helping 'em along. To work twelve hours a day, with half-an-hour pause for dinner, and naught but kicks up the backside if they didn't keep up wi' the brick-makers. Great gobs of clay these little wenches had to carry, from the puddling-pool to the work-benches. Big hefty women, bare footed, puddling the clay, treading it to the right mixture, like making wine. Only the pictures I'd seen of the peasants treading the grapes were happy ones, wi' smiles on faces and delight in the work. Clay-puddling was never like

57

that. Wet and cold and miserable. And the little wenches would heft the clay to the brick-making women, two loads at a time. Twenty pounds o' wet clay stuck on their heads, then they'd have to stoop down and clutch another twenty pounds to their bellies, and carry the lot to the brick-maker.

'Ah worked it out,' Gyp said, 'each little wench would carry about seven tons o' clay in a work-stent. No wonder most of 'em died afore they'd seen thirty years . . . no wonder many on 'em had rickets and twisted bloody spines.'

'But why was it so?' I wanted to know, 'why'd they let it be so?'

'Who's *they*?'

'Well. Moms and dads and teachers and—and gaffers, and—and—and governments.'

Gyp laughed. No joy in the laughter. A bark more than a laugh.

'Moms and dads couldn't do anything about things,' he told me. 'They were glad enough to tek the three shillings the kids 'ould put on the table come Saturday dinner-time. Most of that would get pissed up against the pub wall Sat'day night, any road. And teachers wouldn't protest because there *was* no teachers for the likes of them. If yo' wanted education, yo' paid for it. And if yo' could afford for yo're kids to tek schooling yo' didn't put 'em in brick-yards or nail-shops or pits. Yo' educated 'em and turned 'em into gaffers to mek other kids do the bloody work.'

'What about the gaffers and governments, then? Why didn't they tek some heed of what it was like, then?' I protested.

'Gaffers and governments bist the same thing, then as now,' Gyp answered me. 'Get the most out'n folks for the least outlay. Hosses had it better—hosses had doctor-vets to traipse round 'em every time they farted, and clean straw for beds, and good fittle to feed on.'

'It was all wrong,' I said, 'all wrong.'

'Wrong it was and wrong it still is,' Gyp agreed, 'better now than then in some roads . . . but still bad. Still bloody deep-down black bad.'

'Is that why you won't get a job, Gyp? Even if there was work to go to? If there was no dole-queues?'

'Ah reckon so.'

'You could have lots of things, Gyp. You'n got a good head on yo're shoulders, folks say.'

He stopped in mid-stride, staring not outwards but inwards.

'Sithee,' he said, quiet-voiced but with power in the voice, 'all ah want—all ah *ever* wanted—is to *be*. Me, complete. Not an extension of a system I detest and abhor. Not to have social betters or un-betters and stuff like that. Not to be gaffer or be gaffered. But above all, not to be exploited.'

'What's exploited mean, then?'

He looked at me long and then grinned, and then laughed.

'It's what yo'll be when yo' grows up,' he said, 'unless a bit of me rubs off on you.'

We started walking again. The canal flanked us, with the two dirty iron boats being loaded with bricks. Wenches brought the loaded carts to the cut-side, and a couple of men took 'em from there and stacked them in the damp holds. The boat-horses cropped clover and sweet grass against the time they'd be needed. An arched bridge spanned the cut so that one part of the brick-yard was joined to the other, and the cut splitting down the middle of both bits.

Gyp took my attention to the bridge-arch.

'See them bricks?' he directed me, 'they'm called Blue Bricks. The whole world meks no better nor them. Hard bricks, the best. The wind will never wear 'em down, nor water. They'll last as long as time itself and that's a fact. Special to this region, bist Blue Bricks. The old-time cut-men and railroad builders knew the value of these 'uns. Rennie, Telford, Brunel, Stevenson. They used hundreds and thousands on 'em for their bridge-building all over the country. And yo' listen to me. Brunel and Telford and Stevenson and them, they got the glory for building these bridges. They got the medals and the pats on the heads. History books in school lauds and praises 'em. Yet each and every one on 'em should have been stood agin a wall and shot, straight in the belly so's they'd die slow.'

59

I was aghast.

'Why, Gyp? Why?'

'Because they built their glory on the misery of too many wenches and lads, men and women. Because every Blue Brick they laid was a monument to bloody awful misery. Because they exploited worse than plantation slave-drivers, and chalked it all up to private gain and public glory. There's descendants of the Brunels and the Stevensons of this world still wallowing in the luxuries left 'em by their forbears, never having lifted a hand to earn a penny on it. They should have the lot tekken from 'em and split up among old brick-workers who bist in the workhouse, f'rinstance.'

I felt uneasy inside, because what Gyp was telling me was making our history teacher out to be a liar. She told us that the railway and canal 'giants' were great men, and Gyp was telling me they were filthy piddle in a pool.

'Yo' know something?' Gyp asked me, 'burn this bit in yo're mind. When Queen Victoria came through this region she had the curtains of her railway carriage drawn shut, so's not to see the horrors of the Black Country.'

'Should she have bin shot, then?'

'No,' Gyp answered, 'her should have bin dragged here and made to work a twelve-hour stent for the rest of her bloody un-natural life.'

He rolled one of his thin cigarettes.

'Enough on it,' he said, blowing smoke, 'let's get on wi' what we'n come for.'

'What'n yo' want the bricks for?' I asked him, 'these seconds you'm going to see about?'

'Build a pig-sty.'

'Where's the pig, then?'

'Haven't got one yet. First things first.'

'Why'd yo' want a pig, then?'

'To fatten and feed and feast on, you silly bugger.'

'Ar, then,' I said.

'Ah'm not queueing for free soup,' he said, 'nor bist I going cap in hand to Means Test for a grocery ticket to feed me and my mam. Not after bully-beef and bullets, ah bisn't. We'll live on what ah can grow in my allotment, or take from the land. Ah'm returning to the ways of my great-great-grand-feyther, the last of the Green Countrymen ah was telling you about.'

We were well into the brick-yard now. It was like as if a huge blow-lamp had been lit fierce and then swung round in a circle, destroying everything the flame reached, turning it into a circle of desolation. The fields and grass and bramble-bushes and weeds grew straight up to the edge of the huge circle, then ended abruptly, just like Teacher wiping a black-board duster through the middle of a word. As abrupt and unexpected as that. And as sharply untidy.

Round the edges of the yard bricks were stacked, all baked and finished and waiting to be carried off by hoss-cart or lorry, or cut-boats. Hundreds and thousands of house-bricks. Pyramids of them. They were stacked in hard compact wedges, each wedge the size of a bungalow. Beyond these were oblong-shaped archway-bricks, chimney-cowlings, roof-tiles and other odds and sods I couldn't put names to or purpose to. I didn't like any of them. They had no colour or movement, only a barren lack of both. I could see mostly women working the bricks; just one or two men were there, but mostly women. I walked close to Gyp as we passed by the rows of baking-ovens, ready to climb into his pocket if one of the women was so much as to look at me.

He sensed me.

'They bist only wenches,' he said, 'they wusn't bloody bite you.'

'It's yo' they'm looking at,' I muttered, 'not at me.'

'Ar, then,' he said, grinning and winking.

The women and wenches worked hard, not furiously. There was a man-drive about them. They worked like men, with the same ease-deliberation, the same unwastage of movement— every non-essential movement was missing. So instead of being a bit jerky like it sometimes was at the picture-house when the fillums were a bit on the old and slow side, there was a sort of harmony to all they did. Like as if everything had been practised and rehearsed time after time 'til it was movement-perfect. But despite they knew all the short-cuts to prevent over-sweating, nearly all of them *were* sweating. It wasn't work, it was graft. Man-graft. Gyp must'a' read my thoughts.

'After a day's work,' he said, 'they'n still got a day's work to do. Cooking dinner for their men and families, washing and ironing. Cleaning the house up.' He grinned faintly.

'It's wimmen like them as makes blokes like me like wimmen like them,' he said, and I think it was a sort of compliment.

'They works hard as men,' he said, 'and the gaffers pay 'em half as much money. They'll tek wimmen on the pay-roll but not men. So the wimmen has to do it, tek what comes, to put food into bellies.'

The women were work-sweaty when you came near them, and you could smell it. Those working the ovens and in the direct heat of things were dripping wet, and were peeled down to bloomers and slips to catch the most coolness. A few, not many, were showing their titties. All uncovered they were, and as they worked and heaved beard-bushes of hair showed from their arm-pits. I felt myself blushing and tried hard not to stare at their titties. But I did stare and when they caught me at it they turned away so's I shouldn't see, sort of modest and secret. Many of the women called out to Gyp, the young wenches especially. When they saw him they suddenly stopped being close relations to work-hosses, and became female. Some of them were very pretty under their work-dirt, and seeing Gyp made them shine with womanhood and some sort of grace that was lacking when they hadn't been aware of him. He gave a word and a grin to each and every one of them, and as he passed down the long line of ovens they stopped at their work to stare after him. One wench blushed bright scarlet when he looked at her, and went inside a cold-oven to hide.

'Yo've bin theer, then, Gyp,' an older woman called, seeing the little scene, 'dipped yo're stick in the honey-pot, it looks like.'

I couldn't figure the meaning of what she said; it puzzled me.

'Yo' doesn't keep bees, Gyp,' I said loudly, 'what's she mean about dipping yo're stick in the honey pot, then?'

I'd said something funny, because all the women who were nearby burst into peals and cackles of laughter, and the wench hiding inside the oven wouldn't come out.

Gyp singled out one of the few men about the yard, crossed to him.

'How bist, Gyp,' the man said.

'How bist,' Gyp answered.

'What can ah do for thee?'

'Ah'd like a few bricks. Seconds. To build a sty with. And two three-feet long half-pipes to make troughs from. A hundred and thirty bricks.'

The man shook his head.

'Ah dussn't,' he said, 'the gaffer would lay me off if ah gave you bricks.'

'Ah can manage ten shillings.'

The man was surprised.

'For that much, yo' can go straight into the office and place the order yourself,' he said, 'they'll deliver to yo're house for ten shillings.'

'Ar,' Gyp answered, 'that and no more. What ah'm getting at, Jim, is that ah'll give yo' the ten shillings. For five hundred bricks—seconds—and twelve feet of half-gutter.'

'Thought yo' only wanted a hundred-and-thirty, and six feet?'

'If ah go to the office that's all ah'll get for my ten bob— enough to make one sty. If yo' look after me, I's'll be able to mek three or four sties.'

'Ar, then,' the man said, and thought about it.

'Tell you what,' he said at last, 'ah'll get 'em placed for you— but it's yo're risk to get 'em away from here without dropping me in the shit wi' the gaffer.'

'Fair enough. How long will it take?'

'Few at a time—say a week?'

'Ar, then.'

'This is what ah'll do,' the man explained, 'see that flood-bank just up theer near the bridge?' We could see it. A shallow cut-away which drained the canal water off if it should raise its level high enough to be in fear of flooding the tow-paths, coming over the lips as we called it.

'There's always two-three feet of water left in the flood-cutting,' he said, 'and ah shall put the bricks in there. Yo'll have to fish 'em out for yourselves. Nobody's got reason to go theer, but if they do ah know nothing on it. The gaffers will think the boat-men have chucked part of a load in—ah shall know nothing on it.'

'Fair enough,' Gyp agreed, 'cop this ten shillings, then.' The man took the money.

'Ah'll drink yo're health,' he said.

'Up the workers,' Gyp replied. At the far edge of the brick-yard a man appeared, dressed in good suit and shoes. One of the gaffers.

'He'll have seen thee,' the brick-man said calmly, 'his eyes don't miss the bloody droppings of a pigeon's arse at half a mile. Come over and see it out, Gyp. Ask him for a job, then.'

The three of us approached the gaffer. He waited on our coming not taking a step to come nigh us,

'Mister Jeavens,' the brickman said, 'feller here looking for a job. Ah told him yo' weren't putting anybody on, but thought it best he asked yo' direct. Me not being the ganger like.'

The man looked at Gyp briefly.

'No vacancies,' he said. Gyp nodded and turned away with me in tow.

'Just thought ah'd ask,' he said.

We'd only gone two paces when the gaffer's voice halted us.

'Are you married?' he called after Gyp. 'If your wife has worked in yards, we can manage a place, meybe.'

'Not married,' Gyp answered.

'The lad there with you—if he's on school-leaving, we might fit him in for a year or two.'

'No,' said Gyp, 'he'll not work for thee. I's'll make enough

64

money to send him to a college, so's he can come out and be a gaffer hisself.' We walked from the brick-yard and back into the sweet green fields, and I scuffed the brick-dust from my boots against the grass to get rid of its unpleasantness. Gyp was whistling a tune sweet as a lark, and the notes of it sweetened the sky.

We cut at an angle between coal-pits and brick-yards, coming to wild open spaces of commonland which were clumped with bushes and clusters of trees, and seemed a world apart from anywhere else. We pushed into a thicket, came to a clearing, and Gyp motioned me to sprawl alongside him in the cool grass and held a finger to his mouth for quiet. He took his new pistol from his pocket and examined it carefully. We waited. I could feel cramp-pains nudging into my legs, but as long as Gyp was still and quiet so would I be. One moment the rabbits weren't there and the next they were there. They came out of the opposite thicket, three of them. Even from that distance, thirty feet, I could see that it was a buck and two does. A young-ish buck by the prick of his ears and sheen of his fur. Gyp raised the pistol with both hammers already cocked, he sighted down the long barrels, catching the bead of the front-sights in the 'v'-notch of the rear. He pressed one trigger, then inside a split heart-beat he pressed the other. The pistol made a double noise. Not loud, not cracking out like I'd expected, but a soft noise. Like wet putty being slapped against a piece of wood. The buck and one of the does stayed on the ground, twitching, whilst the third belted for safety. Gyp and me broke our cover and went to the fallen rabbits. The doe was shot through the neck, and the buck had taken the ball dead centre between the eyes. Gyp screwed the metal plugs into the pistol barrels, and gave the weapon over to me.

'Hide it up yo're jersey till we get home,' he said, 'if we'm stopped with the rabbits they mightn't search yo' and find the gun.' He took a clasp-knife from a pocket, opened the big blade up. He slit each rabbit neatly from breast to crotch, exposing the gut-contents. Then he took each rabbit by front and back legs and bent them as if he were arching them like a bow, as if he meant to break their backs. What happened was that the gut-contents, the whole pluck of intestines and innards splurted out onto the ground, leaving the carcases clean and tidy. He sorted among the pluck, cutting out bits and pieces. The hearts and livers and kidneys. He wrapped these in his throat-scarf and placed the small bundle in his pocket.

'Me mam'll soon wash the scarf out,' he said. He opened his jacket and there were big pockets inside it, and he placed a rabbit inside each, then buttoned his jacket again to conceal them.

'One for me and one for yo',' he said, 'ah'll skin 'em back at my house, and yo're mam can mek yo' a rabbit stew for to-night's dinner. We'n got some pearl-barley at our house, we's'll spare you some o' that to thicken the stew.'

He left the rabbits' innards lying where they were for the stoats and carrion birds to feed from.

'Not being kind to the stoats,' he told me, 'only considerate towards meself. If stoats bist hungry, they'll hunt rabbits and leave less for the likes of me.' We walked homewards.

'The gun didn't make much of a bang,' I complained. 'Ah thought it would make a good 'un when yo' shooted it.'

'Tricks of the trade,' he said, 'ah mixed the gunpowder wi' powdered glass.'

'What does that do?'

'It makes the bang quieter. It's a trick ah were taught in the trenches by one of our snipers. The powdered glass mixed in wi' the gunpowder helps make the report of the bullet muffled, sithee. Cuts down the range a lot, but it makes for quietness.'

'You must-a gone to Birmingham to buy the percussion-caps,' I said, 'and you never took me with you.'

'If ah'd a-gone to Birmingham ah'd've took you with me', he answered, 'but ah didn't go so ah didn't take you. I made the percussion caps meself.'

'How?'

'With ammonia and iodine—I made a sort of fulminate. Ah shan't tell you exactly how, 'cos like as not yo'd go and experiment on your own and blow your bloody-self up.'

'Will you show me sometime, then?'

'When you'm older.'

'Can ah shoot the gun before then? Before ah'm older?'

'We'll see,' he said, 'ah'll think on it.'

'Don't think on it too long, Gyp,' I pleaded, 'ah can't wait until I'm older to have a shoot at it.'

He nestled the rabbits more comfortably under his jacket.

'Ar, then,' he said.

5

In the long summer school holidays gaffers of works would sometimes take us on to fill the places of them workers who were taking their year's weekly entitlement of summer holiday. They wouldn't take on men because that meant paying a man's wages, but they'd take one or two of us lads on for pocket-money work. We had to work as hard as them as got full wages, but that didn't seem to matter. Some men in work wouldn't take their week's holiday at all, wanting to keep on the gaffer's good side in case he started laying men off. Gyp said that there were two men in the dole-queues for every man in work. He said if every man would drop his tools and walk off the job, the Government would soon do something about the rest of 'em . . . but what the Government would have done to right things, Gyp didn't say.

Sometimes we could get a bit of holiday-work in the iron foundries, other times in the glass-works. We weren't allowed to work in the brick-yards nor in the coal-pits—and by rights, if we earned money from the glass or the iron, our out-of-work dad's were supposed to report it at the Labour Exchange or to the Means Test, so's what we earned could be deducted from their pick-up money. But the foundry and glass-works were pretty good that way. If we said nothing, nor would they. Gyp used to laugh at this and tell me that the gaffer's weren't keeping quiet to be on the kind side, but because they were bloody well ashamed of what they were paying lads for nine-hour stents. Ten shillings a week, from Monday morning to Sat'day dinner-time.

'Will yo' come then?' I asked Noggie. 'Will you come wi' me to the glass-works gaffer and see if he'll set us on for a week or two?'

'What for, then?'

'Earn a bit of money.'

'Me dad gives me a bit of pocket money every Friday.'

'Yo'm lucky, then. Mine don't.'

'Ah can get by wi'out grafting in the glass-works.'

'Like ah said, lucky yo'. I'm off, then.'

I waited for him.

'Ah don't fancy it,' he told me, 'not being cooped up in the glass-works in that heat for all that time. What say we get our bikes out and pedal round the streets looking for loads of coal to get in? We could earn maybe a shilling a ton.'

'There's full-grown blokes already doing that, and they bist charging ninepence a ton. Me own dad's out doing that for a lark.'

'We can offer to do it for sixpence a ton, then.'

'Ninepence the ton's the going price. I's'll not undercut my own feyther.'

I walked off to the glassworks. Noggie followed me more with friendship's duty than enthusiasm.

'I can give the two on you a week as tekkers-in,' the gaffer said to us, the pair of us standing to attention in front of his office desk and trying to look like a glass-works couldn't function without the two of us, 'on morning shifts. Start at har'-past five in the morning and work through 'til two o'clock, half-an-hour for break. Monday to Saturday. Can you get up early enough o' mornings for that?' We nodded.

'Ar, alright,' he said, 'ah'll tek you across into the shop and show yo' which chairs yo'll be working with.' He stood up and we followed him across the high-walled yard into the glass-works itself. The shop was a huge circular building, like the inside of a giant well, made up of bricks. There were a few windows stuck into the walls and the windows could be opened at an angle so that a cold wind wouldn't blow onto the hot glass direct and crack it. The walls sloped inwards and upwards, narrowing in tight high up, so that it was all like a big tun-dish turned upside down. In the middle of the works was a furnace with lots of little holes staring out like hot eyes. The hotness came from the molten glass inside the furnace.

I already knew my way about the glass-works, so it wasn't over-strange. On my way home from school I often stopped by the arched-doorways to stare inside and watch the men making glass.

The gaffer took me and Noggie across to the far side of the shop, paused at a man sitting in his work-bench. The bench had two long arms sticking out in front of it, and across these two arms the man had a long iron rod which he kept rolling backwards and forwards, while he shaped the molten glass which was stuck like treacle to one end. 'Which one o' these two dos't want as tekker-in 'til yo're chap comes back from holiday, Walt?' the gaffer asked him. The man grunted at his work, never taking his eyes from the job he was doing.

'Either one 'ull do me, gaffer,' he said, 'just as long as he'll werk and don't play the idle-sod.'

'Yo' stop with him,' the gaffer said to me, and took Noggie off to the next man and left him there. I stood watching my bloke finish off the water-jug he was making. By the time he'd finished it the red-hotness had left it, and it glowed only amber-warm, almost as if there was no heat left in it. It looked cool enough to pick up, but I knew if you did try to pick it up it would burn your hands down to the bone. Walt stood up from his chair, walked over to a trough lined with asbestos, laid the end of the iron containing the jug over it. He rapped the iron-pole a sharp rap with the steel scissors he carried, and the jug parted company with the iron and lay in the trough. Walt motioned me over to him. He gave me a pair of wooden tongs and a wooden pole which had a 'Y' at one end, like a catapult.

'These'm yo're tools,' he told me, 'yo're tekking-in tools. Do

70

it like this. For jugs, put one end of yo're pole inside the jug. Careful not to knock it about—the jug, not the pole—although it amounts to the same thing in the end. Bad tools means bad work. Now use the tongs to mek sure the jug is secure on the pole. When yo' lift it, lift it like this—upwards, so's it won't fall off and smash on the floor. Dos't see?'

I nodded.

'Right then. When yo've picked it up like ah've shown thee, yo' has to carry it to that place over there. The Lear, it's called. It's an annealing oven. Come on and I's'll show thee.'

I followed him. When we got to the lear I saw that it had got a moving bottom, a sort of belt ever moving away from you as you stood there, moving easy and slow. Walt placed the jug on to the start of the moving belt, pushed it upright with the tongs, and I watched the object creep away from me. It passed between asbestos curtains which lifted for it to enter the long annealing oven, and then it was gone from view.

'That's easy enough then, bisn't it?' Walt asked me, and I nodded again.

'Ah'm on jugs all day,' he said, 'so there's little more to learn than what ah've shown thee. Every different shape has to be carried in a different way, and I's'll show you how to carry as I makes 'em. Now come on back to my chair and ah'll explain. Can't spend too much time explaining, though, 'cos ah bist on piece-work. We'll go through it quick.'

He sat down at his wooden bench, reached down besides it and fetched up a bottle of cold tea. He drank from it, wiped the neck with his hand then passed it across to me for me to take a swig. I just sipped from it for politeness's sake, then gave it back to him.

'This bit of wood ah'm sitting on,' he said, 'it's took me twenty years to get to sit here. Nobody sits in this chair but me. It's not a ornament, it's not a piece of furniture to put yo're arse on. It's a work-tool and it's *mine* and anybody other than me 'ud get away with it better by putting his arse on the King's throne than on this. *It's* called the Chair and the blokes like me are called the Chairmen, meaning we'm top-craftsmen. Mostly we gets called the Workmen. Ah'm *yo're* Workman whilst yo' bist here. The team ah've got werking for me is known as 'a chair o' workmen', and they'm called a Chair for short. Is all this sinking into yo're head?'

'Yes,' I said, because it was.

'Ar, then. Yo'll pick the rest on it up as yo' goes along. Just remember two things—tek 'em in as fast as ah drops 'em into that trough, and don't let me catch you with yo' arse in my chair.'

'Lear', 'Chair', 'Tek-'em in' . . . a new language to learn, and only three words of it yet committed to memory and understanding. Before the day was over I was to add to my vocabulary extensively, with a few cuss-ones sprinkled in for good measure.

Walt, my Chairman, wasn't as hard as he sounded. He didn't work me at *too* hard a pace—at least, I think not. It seemed to take him a long time to make his jug, and I had to stand by until he dropped each one into the asbestos trough, then I'd pick it up on my wooden tongs and pole and walk it down to the lear. Here and there my curiosity led me to ask questions, like why use wooden tools to 'tek-in' with, why not iron ones?

'Iron would scratch the metal,' Walt said, 'once it was away from my hands. It's sort of soft, until it gets annealed. The wooden tools yo' bist using are made from pear-wood, and yo'll notice that although it gets a bit scorched, it doesn't burn like ordinary wood.' I had noticed, but his information impressed me.

'Why do you call glass "metal", then?' I asked him. 'Why?'

'It *is* metal,' he answered. 'It's always called metal in the glass-trade. It's one of the hardest metals there is; that's why it bosts so easy if yo' don't manage it right.'

There were four of us in our gang, or 'chair', with Walt as gaffer over it. After a bit I'd got it figured out. These chair-gaffers called Workmen weren't promoted to their positions like other gangers or foremen. They earned their own promotion over long years applied to their trade, and it was only their ability as top-grade craftsmen which got them into that chair. Once there, nothing could lift them from it unless they forsook

72

their craftsmanship and turned shoddy and careless ... which Walt said had never happened in his whole experience, nor in his dad's nor his grand-dad's.

'Only the slowing down that comes wi' old age meks a craftsman give up his chair,' Walt told me, 'and short o' that, only death.' His hands, with steel cutters and pear-wood tongs, seemed to caress the metal glowing on the end of his iron rod as he stroked it up and down the arms of his chair.

Besides Walt and me there were two other men in our chair. The one man was called the 'footmaker', or sometimes the 'gatherer'. He used a long blow-iron, about five feet long it was with a brass mouthpiece like a trumpet to blow through. A hole ran all the way in the centre of the iron. He dipped these blow-irons into one of the portholes set in the main furnace, twirled the end between his fingers until he'd got a lump of molten metal stuck to the rod. All the time his hands had to keep twisting and twirling, setting up a sort of centrifugal force to keep the glowing mass settled, otherwise it would drop off the end like a blob of thin honey. He never seemed to make a mistake wi' the amount he fetched out'n the furnace. Always just enough for the job intended, no less and no more—and yo' can't weigh molten metal on scales like a chunk of cheese, and cut off what you don't want. When he'd gathered enough glass on his iron he blew gently down the pipe so that the glass itself swelled like a small balloon. When he'd got it to the size he wanted, he passed it to the Chairman, Walt, who's skill was needed to coax and flatter it into the shape wanted. All round us other chairs worked away, some making wine-glasses, others vases, tumblers, and eyes-know-what.

The other bloke with us was a sort of odd-job man. He was called the 'sticker-up'. He used a slim solid rod called a pontil or a punty, and with this he supplied small quantities of metal for Walt to make such things as wine-glass feet, or, as now, jug-handles.

Now and then I passed Noggie on his way to or back from the lear.

'Be-Christ, it's bloody hot in here,' was all the words he'd say.

73

And it *was* hot. Sucking-hot. Heat all round, like blankets pressed close on a summer night. In between taking-in the finished jugs for Walt I had a good chance to look around me at the other chairs. The men were all pale-skinned, white-skinned, wi' no sun-tan or weather-colour to them like Gyp or the Steersman. I s'pose it was through working in the heat all the time; the skin of them couldn't get itself an undercoat for the sun to paint itself on.

I liked the colours inside the glass-works—I didn't like the heat, but I liked the colours. They reminded me of the pictures Teach had shown us in school, some pictures by a painter called Rembrandt and another called Titty-an, or something. Their pictures all had this sort of warm-glow, as if the firelight from and russets, warm and somehow inviting. The faces in the pictures all had this sort of warm-glow, as if the firelight from an ash-grid were reflecting on to them. The glass-workers all had this sort of glow on them. From the over-spill light thrown by the central furnace, or from the more direct light of the molten glass they were working into shape. The heat-light carved warm shades and lightnesses into their faces, and I felt I'd like to draw a frame round each one and tek it away with me and hang on my bedroom wall to keep looking at. It was when you got outside into the fresh air that you noticed how pale of skin the glass-workers were, white as dead fish floating belly upwards in the cut.

I was pleased enough when the work's-hooter blew the signal for an half-hour's stop. Noggie didn't come over to me. I saw him sprawl out under a window as if he were going to have a nap.

'What makes glass, Mr Walt?' I asked my Workman. 'It doesn't just grow—where does it come from, then?'

'From the good earth,' he told me seriously, 'from the good earth. Silver sand and red lead, and other stuff. A dash of arsenic. Every glass-works gaffer has got his own trade-secrets o' mixing glass in its batch-stage . . . but the sands of the earth bist general all round. Sieve it, mix it, melt it and make it.'

'The furnace must be as hot inside as the sun.'

'One thousand three hundred and sixty degrees *cent*igrade,'
Walt said precisely, emphasising the 'cent' bit, 'that's the heat
of the furnace exactly. Always kept at that.'

The figure groped at my mind. I gave it up. Must be at least
as hot as a kettle on the boil, I thought.

'Do we make good glass round here?' I asked. 'Is it well
thought on?'

'The best in the world,' he answered, 'bar none. Stourbridge
cut glass—Black Country table-glass. There comes no better.'

I was pleased.

'Ah'm glad o' that,' I said sincerely, 'ah really am glad.'

A smile broke his stern face up and made him look years
younger.

'Ah'm pleased that yo'm glad, young 'un,' he answered,
'that's the nicest thing ah've heard said in a long time. Yo'
listen to me—come into glass when you leaves school. There'll
be room, then. Things will have picked up ... come here wi'
me and I's'll teach you all that ah know. My word's on it.' He
took a sandwich from his fittle-bag and bit on it. 'Hasn't got
any snap with thee?' he asked, surprised, 'no fittle to chew
on?'

'We came for a job on the off-chance.' I explained, em-
barrassed for having no food. 'The gaffer put us straight on.
There was no chance to go home and get a piece out'n the
pantry.'

He dug into his fittle bag, pulled out a couple of thick-wedge
sandwiches and handed them to me.

'Get this down thee,' he ordered. 'There's enough here for
the two on us.'

The clock on the wall said we'd got fifteen minutes' dinner-
time left yet.

'I's'll give you a tip,' Mr Walt said to me. 'When yo' starts
working in the glass-works for the first time, it tires you. The
heat tires you, not the work. It's not hard work, not heavy. But
it's tiring. Yo' sweats your strength out, that's the trouble.
Sweating means you'm losing body salt and that's precious. So
for the first few days, till you'm acclimatised, drink a spoonful

of salt in water every two-three hours. It'll keep you strong. Nasty taste, but mark my words, it'll fettle you up.'

He pointed to his tool-locker.

'Packet o' salt in there,' he said, 'just help yourself. Mark what I say.'

He was right. I drank the salt and water every two hours, regular and bitter as medicine. I told Noggie to do the same but he scoffed.

'Salt meks yo' thirsty,' he said, 'any bloody fool knows that.' He looked nearly washed up, did Noggie.

My head was reeling with information yet to be filed and stored away, by the time knocking-off time came. I never knew there was so much bloody glass in the world, or kinds. Drinking-glass, bottle-glass, window-glass, soda-class, flint-glass, crystal-glass . . . I'd never remember all I was told, I thought. And the glass-makers were only part of things, because after him there was the glass-cutter. But my feeling was that not a lot of love was lost between glass-maker and glass-cutter. They worked in different parts of the yard, had their own language and separate skills, and each thought he was better than t'other. The glass-makers gave me the impression that glass-cutters were nought but bloody nuisances who mutilated *their* work— the glass-maker's—with cuts and designs and things. The glass-maker liked to think that the object which left his chair and hands was perfect in itself, in every way, wi'out some other man laying hands to it and trying to 'improve' it.

I lost count of how many times I walked to and from the lear (Walt said it was spelled 'Lehr' but didn't tell me why) and when the stent was due to end I was tired enough. I'd already made up my mind that ah didn't want to be a glass-man when I left school because no matter how beautiful and lovely the stuff was that they made, I reckoned it would get a bit boring to have to do it year in and year out. It'd become just another job, tied to the clock on the works-wall, with a hooter shouting the odds when you could stop for a bit of a break. Didn't seem right, to me, that the good work of a man's hands and mind should be governed in that way. Gyp had told me that the

Black Country was Green Country, once, and all its people were agricultural workers, working the herds and the flocks and the fields. It seemed a far cry from that to now . . . but as I watched the glass-men at work I couldn't help but think there *was* a link between them and their forbears. It was there in their steady deliberateness, in the way their hands and eyes seemed to be half a step ahead of the job being done, as if measuring its coming along. And the fact that the stuff that made glass was taken from the earth, from the soil their forbears—and mine—tilled and planted. It seemed to me, quick and sudden-like, that the glass objects they made were fruits, glowing fruits, taken from an orchard once they were ripe. The thought on it pleased me and I tucked it away under a crease of my mind to tell Gyp later.

The men cleaned their tools and collected their home-going bits and pieces. Some of them sluiced their faces at the water-bosh. Noggy looked as limp as wilted celery. I swilled my face and hands at the water-bosh along with the men, but Noggie didn't. He sprawled out on the floor near a window, gasping like a floundering fish. He was bloody-well full-spent and worn out, but me—I'd still got a bit of freshness left to me. I listened happily to the banter of the men around me.

'Christ,' one of them said, 'but it's welly-bloody hot.'

'Hark at him,' a mate murmured, 'complains about the heat and when he gets home and finds his missus has let the fire out he gives her a bloody belting.'

Another of them was trying to wedge his empty tea-bottle into a jacket pocket. The pocket must have been cluttered up with other rubbish, 'cos it was a tight fit.

'Yo' wants to get a littler bottle, Tommy,' my Workman said to him, 'a smaller one would do it.'

Tommy stared at him with mock-glumness.

'No need, Walt,' he said, 'ah shall just tell me mam not to fill it so full in the morning.'

I walked home with Noggie.

'God spare me days,' he grumbled, mourning and shuffling like an old grey man, 'but if that's work yo' can keep it. Ah'd rather rob a bleeding bank to earn my carrots.'

I left him on his doorstep.

'I's'll call for thee at three o'clock,' I said, 'after ah've had me dinner. We'll go off down the cut and see how the Steersman's coming along wi' his new boat, if you like.'

Noggie stared at me blankly.

'Ah'm not coming out to play,' he said, 'ah'm going to bed. Ah'm that tired ah could sleep the clock round.'

'You'm a weakling,' I said, sneering, 'an ounce of work and yo'm flat out.'

'Bring me day's wages back wi' yo' tomorrow,' he said sleepily, ignoring my taunts, 'because ah'm not going back *theer* again. It's too bloody hot in there—ah might end up in hell, but ah'm buggered if ah bist going before ah'm sent for.'

❧ 6 ❧

I worked with Walt and his chair for four days and was almost dead on my feet at the end of 'em, despite the salt and water. Walt took a special interest in me, saying he'd put a word in for me with the gaffers when I left school.

'Gaffers aren't putting men on,' he told me, 'but they'll put school-leavers on. See, they'n got to *train* some newcomers, otherwise they'll have no workers when things settle and trade picks up again.'

I made my face look enthusiastic, but I knew ah wouldn't be coming into glass when I left school.

'Ah knew yo'd got it in you,' Walt told me, 'the moment yo' started asking questions. An enquiring mind you'n got. Not like yo're mate—he never come back after that first day, did he? Hasn't got the sap, he hasn't.'

I felt loyalty towards Noggie welling inside me.

'He would've come back,' I defended, 'only he's poorly. Someat upset his belly and he's a-bed.'

At the end of the fourth day the gaffer came up to us, and put me in another department for finishers on Friday and Saturday.

'I's'll have to tek him away from you, Walt,' the gaffer said, 'we'm five lads short in the cutting-shop. We need somebody a bit bright in there to fill a gap. Yo'll have to mek do wi' sharing a tekker-in with two or three other chairs.'

Walt didn't like it.

'Ah'n got this 'un half trained, gaffer,' he complained. 'He's coming along like sunshine under me.'

But his objections were soft-spoken. He didn't want to upset his boss, not in times like we were in he didn't.

'Come back and work wi' me,' Walt called as I went away with the gaffer. 'Yo' come back to me when yo' can, and I's'll make a glass-worker out'n you.'

I walked with the gaffer across the yard until we came to the cutting-shops. Long white-washed barns of places, full of noise and clutter. There were twenty cutting-lathes in two lines, facing each other. Each glass-cutter was sitting on a wooden stool, cutting glass on a wheel which spinned on an axle. Back of this wheel was a work-bosh for each cutter, like two rows of coffins they looked like, about the same size and shapes of coffins. Running up from each cutting belt, up to the ceiling, where it joined another long thick spinning-shaft, was a leather strap. It was this strap, turned by the main shaft, which made the cutting wheels turn. On the main drive-shaft, at each end, were huge iron wheels, just like wheels off a railway engine, which seemed to turn slowly: balancing wheels, like fly-wheels inside a clock. The noise was regular, slap-slap of the leather belts, rumble-rumble of the drive shafts, squeak-squeak and rasp-rasp of the cutting wheels against the glass. Under this main noise I could hear the fainter noises of men singing to themselves, or cussing as something went wrong wi' what they were doing. They couldn't talk with each other, only to themselves, because of the fuller and heavier noise all round them. The gaffer took me to one end of the main-shop to where glassware of every sort was stacked, waiting to be cut.

'Ah want you to keep the cutters fed wi' work,' he told me. 'Yo'll see that each man is kept stocked up. As the cutters finish cutting, take away from 'em and stack carefully over there. Keep 'em filled up from these piles. See what sort of glass each one bist working on, and feed him the same. Just be careful, chap. Go easy and gentle with 'em . . . glass is fragile and won't stand bouncing about.'

He left me to it, and I saw straight off that I wasn't being called on to work as hard as I'd worked in the glass-making part. Nor was there the same heat to contend with. Everything moved at a slower rate, and I'd got time to look round me and watch what was going on. I watched the men decorating the glass. They made rough cuts first, wi' emery wheels, then blue-grey coloured smoothing wheels to take out the white coarseness of the first cuts. Two men were decorating the wares with engraving wheels which were made out of copper, and kept to a smooth cutting edge with oil dripping down a quill on to the wheel itself. Every so often the engravers wiped the oil from the glass and held it up to the light, eyes screwed up critically, looking for faults or blemishes in their own work. These men were artists—I'd half made up my mind I'd come into glass after all and be one of 'em. They cut pictures into the glass, not designs. Birds and things—horses and chariots and ferns and flowers, trees and animals. One man was actually cutting a portrait of somebody into the glass, and the picture he cut was as good as or better than a portrait our Art Master could draw at school. Standing near the bench of this man was a two-foot high vase with a whole picture-story cut into it; horsemen and hounds streaming after a fox, all round the vase it lasted, until you could see the foremost dog's nose touching the fox's tail. If your wits didn't tell you the truth of matters, you'd think it was the fox chasing the dogs and horsemen. . . . But it was a beautiful picture; that real you half expected animals and men to come off the glass and go racing across the floor, stream out of the doorway and into the sunlight. The hands of the glass-cutters were slow and easy in movement, almost like ladies' hands. They looked pale and soft, and as they turned the glass this way and that to cut it it reminded me of our music teacher in assembly when she waved her hands like wands to conduct the music.

One man could tell his work from another man's, no matter if each were doing the same sort of job and they were all mixed up together. It was like each man had put a secret *feel* into his work, so that his hands knew it again the moment he touched it. They cut diamonds into the glass, trellis-works and lattices,

81

stars and bevels. Water dripped on to their cutting wheels to
stop them from getting heated up, and the work-boshes were
filled with water to a few inches level, and under the water was
a thick white sort of sand that was heavy and funny to feel. The
cutters told me that the 'white sand' was really powdered glass
mixed up with grains of emery-wheels, and I mustn't get any
into my mouth because if it got into my belly it would sand-
paper my guts down to my backbone. As they finished cutting
the objects I took them away and gave them new stuff to cut.
The finished jobs were taken away to another shed, where men
worked in rubber aprons and gloves and wellingtons, dipping
the glass into lead-troughs that were filled with strong-smelling
acid. The cut-glass bowls and vases and drinking glasses went
into the acid dull and lacking lustre, but when they came out of
the acid they were shining bright and the cut-patterns threw
light at your eyes like star-bursts and rainbows. They seemed to
glow, with hints of blueness in the cuts and diamond-whiteness.
They looked good and splendid, and I couldn't help being
proud inside that these things were made *here*, where I was
born and raised.

The gaffer didn't seem like a gaffer when he looked at the
glass his men had made and cut. He seemed like a man in a
private, pleasant dream. I watched him a time or two when he
came into the cutting-shop on some errand or other, and he'd
go to the finished stuff which was already acid-polished and
waiting to be packed and sent off. He'd take a vase, rest it on a
smooth surface, then ping it with the knuckle of a finger. And
you could hear the bell-sound ringing out wave after wave . . .
as if each throb of bell-sound built up a wave behind itself to
make another, so that the sound went on and on, fading slowly,
like music-teacher's tuning-fork—only better and more beautiful, a sort of music you wanted to make your throat fit and
imitate, like Gyp imitating a bird-song. The gaffer would ring
it, mouth smiling, eyes dreaming a bit. He'd hold it up to the
light and catch the colours dancing from the cuts and patterns,
let his fingers whisper round the goodness of it. And me, too,
looking . . . I forgot the heat and sweat that'd made the object,

forgot the men with the punty-irons and blow-irons, the sun-hot furnace where the batch got melted. I could only see the finished loveliness of it all, and it seemed to have nothing to do wi' workmen and wages and hard times or good. The glass seemed always to have been, like flowers have always been, and kingfishers down the cut with fire in their wings and crests when the sunlight caught 'em in it.

'It's good stuff,' the gaffer said, speaking to himself more than to me. 'It comes no better. Not like your foreign bloody rubbish, full o' mistakes and shoddiness. Most people other than glass-men wouldn't notice the defects . . . but ah do.' He looked at me and spoke direct to me. 'I notice,' he said, 'because all my life has been spent in glass. Spent among the best craftsmen in the bloody world, young 'un—men who'll accept nowt but the best. Tek foreign glass and hold it up to the light and yo'll see bits of carbo-paste left in the cuts, not tekken out by the smoothing wheels. See crossed diamonds wheer the points don't meet—or worse still, actually cut across each other. See foot-stars which don't meet smack-on to the centre. Vases who's lip-edges have been bevel-cut to hide a crack. The way to test 'em is ping 'em with a finger. If the sound's flat and dead, not gooin' on forever, then it's no bloody good. Back into the cullet-bin wi' it, and melt it down for next time.' I didn't understand half of what he was saying, but I nodded and looked wise at him.

'Ar, then,' the gaffer said, 'what ah'm telling yo' is right. But let me tell thee this and all—if diamond be king of decorative beauty, then cut glass bist first prince to it. Diamond already exists, but man has to take white sand and red lead oxide, salt-petre and magnesia, and make the first prince—glass. Dos't thee understand?'

I nodded.

He nodded approvingly.

'Come and see me when yo' leaven school,' he said, 'ah'm allus on the look-out for a sharp apprentice, no matter what the times bist like.' But out of all he'd told me only one thing stuck in my mind. Saltpetre. I couldn't wait to get to Gyp, to tell him that he could get saltpetre from the glass-works to mek his gunpowder. Gunpowder to go into the pistol, mine and his'n.

I felt excited inside, as if I'd got a parcelled present to give to Gyp wi' my own two hands. And then the excitement went away as I realised that Gyp was bound to be a hundred steps in front of me, and that he'd already know for sure that he could get saltpetre in glass-works; and, knowing him, like as not he'd already got a ton of it salted away some place. There was prob'ly nothing I could tell Gyp that he didn't already know, and the thought on it made a sour little niggle inside my mind. One day, I thought, I's'll come up with something he *doesn't* know, and *that*'ll impress him.

Sat'day dinner time came and I collected my wages; ten shillings less three-pence for the 'works fund', whatever that might've been, and I wasn't sorry to see the work behind me. I'd done a week's stent and hadn't seen Gyp or the Steersman, or even Noggie since the first work-day. I might as well have been at the other end of the country for all I'd seen of 'em. I took my money home and kept a shilling for spenders, and went round to Noggie's house. He was sprawled out in the kitchen with a parcel of old comics in front of him, eyes popping as he followed a story in pictures.

'Yo'm finished wi' work, then?' he asked me, and I nodded, clutching my proud shilling in my pocket. I'd changed the shilling piece for twelve pennies at the grocery-shop, and the weight of the pennies made me feel light-headed rich.

'How much did yo' get out'n it, then?' he asked.

'Twelve pence.'

'Yo' wants yo're head seeing to,' he answered, 'working guts out for a couple of tanners. My dad give me a shilling for doing nowt but riding wi' him on the pony-cart.'

'You'm lucky, then,' I told him back, 'you'm lucky to have a dad who'll give it. My dad didn't have a smoke all week 'til ah took my bit-money home.'

'Ar, then,' Noggie said indifferently, putting his comics away neatly into a corner of the room, 'what's'll we do, then?'

'Just moach round, ah suppose. See what's doing.'

'Like what?'

'Like anything.'

'Kid's stuff, that is.'

'What is?'

'Moaching is.'

'How'd yo' know until yo've moached?'

'Ah've moached before, and it's boring.'

'Work was boring for yo' as well,' I sneered, 'everything's boring for yo'. Yo'm like a kid—ten minutes of one thing and yo' wants to start on the next.'

'Don't get uppitty,' Noggie said, 'just 'cos yo've earned your-self a shilling bit for a week's donkey-work of sweat and graft ... while ah took it easy and copped a shilling for doing nowt.'

The way he said it, it sounded right, somehow. Like as if he was in the right of things, as if ah'd been made a fool of, at my own fault. It seemed a bit unfair the way things had worked out. Grin and bear it, I said to myself, don't let it show.

'I enjoyed working in glass-works,' I told him airily. 'It were a lot of fun and I learned a lot of things.'

'Ah'm glad,' Noggie said. 'Yo' keep it up. So's gaffers can suck from you what yo've learned, and pay you piddle-pools for doing it.'

I should be saying that, I thought, not Noggie. I should be saying what Noggie's saying because they'm the sort of things that Gyp says.

'We might as well go moaching around,' Noggie said, as if the idea had suddenly come to him and it was a reasonably good one. 'There's nothing else left to do.'

We just let our feet follow the direction our noses were pointed in. We moached into Stourbridge and passed by the Labour Exchange. There was a long queue of men outside and a big notice in the window saying 'NO VACANCIES'. The men were there just to sign on. They all looked like men I'd once seen queueing up for soup and beds outside the Salvation

Army doss-house in Birmingham, down-and-outers. But the men in the dole-queue weren't down-and-outers, they were dad's and brothers and uncles and nephews looking for work ... they were all of them somebody's son or dad or brother. They looked worn and flat, like good dogs that'd been scolded and didn't know what for. Some of them squatted against the Labour Exchange wall, staring like blind men in front of themselves. It all looked sort of musty—they seemed not to be in their own clothes, almost, empty inside their clothes. I felt a sadness for the men, something I couldn't put name to. For a small minute I almost stood inside Gyp's mind and understood what things made him so angry, as if he wanted to swing his fists at somebody or something.

'Don't bloody well stare at them,' I said to Noggie fiercely. 'Leave 'em be.'

'Idle sods,' Noggie said, 'they dinna bloody well want work.'

'There *is* no work for 'em, you saft bugger.'

'There's work if they want it,' Noggie said. 'My dad works and so could they if they wanted.'

'My dad isn't working,' I told him hotly, 'and he wants to work.'

'He'd find work if he looked hard enough,' said Noggie loftily, 'it's just that they'm too bloody bone-idle to look for it.'

I hauled off and hit my mate Noggie on the nose and I saw it splosh like a squashed orange, and the blood was dripping like a tap, and I hauled off and hit him in the eye and he staggered back. He tossed his head to clear the blood and he came at me like a windmill on the move, fists and arms flying, and I copped him again with one on the jaw and it stopped him and rocked him. His full eye and half-closed one looked out at me wild and shocked and I kept my fists waiting for him in case he came back at me.

'Wha—wha' was that for?' he squeaked, tears already gathering, 'whass all that for... ?'

'Because you make me fucking sick,' I screamed, using *the* word out loud and in the same instant waiting for God to come up back of me on tip-toed quietness and swat me into hell.

'Because you'm a bloody monty sod, that's why.'

Across the road some of the men were cheering me on.

'See to him, me lover—put'm on the floor, then.'

'Goo on, little 'un—yo've got him frittened, big as he is.'

Noggie was crying full now. He dabbed a handkerchief at his nose. I envied him that. All I'd got for hanky was a bit of old shirt-tail.

'Yo' can sod off forever,' Noggie told me, turning for home. 'And I's'll tell thee this—just as soon as me eye's bist alright again and me nose stops bleeding ah shall come and give yo' the paling of yo're life.' His voice was muffled under handker-chief.

'Goo on, then,' I jeered after him. 'Yo'm a quitter—ah've bested thee.' I watched him go away, and then felt a bit uneasy in case he told his dad and his dad came after me to belt me a couple. But, I thought, if he does, my dad'll go after *his* dad and belt *him* three or four.

I went looking for Gyp and found him in the backyard of his house, with a cobbler's last wedged in between his knees and an old motor-tyre by him. He'd got a mouthful of cobbler's brads poking from his teeth and they looked like small glinting steel teeth. He spat them into his hand as he saw me, greeted me with his usual 'How bist, chap?' I plonked myself beside him. He studied me.

'Ah'd say yo'n been fighting,' he said, 'judging by the state of yo're knuckles. Hast, then?'

I nodded.

'Who with, then?'

'Me mate. Noggie.'

'M'mm,' he said, 'that's serious bisn't it?'

I told him about it. About what Noggie had said about the Labour Exchange men. Gyp's face went grim.

'Ar, then,' he said, 'ah reckons yo're mate Noggie bloody well asked for it, then. Ah hopes yo' made a good job of thrapin' him.'

'One on the nose, one in the eye, one on the chin,' I said. He grinned.

'One-two-three,' he approved, 'and they dussn't come any better, providing they was good 'uns.'

'They were good 'uns,' I agreed. 'He went home blarting.'

I watched Gyp cut rubber from the lorry tyre, shape a shoe-sole from it. He'd got his rabbit-skinning knife to cut with, and it sliced the tough rubber like it wasn't there. He placed the cut sole onto the shoe, hammered a couple of brads in to hold it fixed. Then he started at the toe and hammered a line of brads all round the edge of the sole, quarter-of-an-inch apart. Then he ran a line of them down the centre. There was a candle with its end grease-glued to the bottom of an upturned jam-jar. He lit it with a match and then took a stick of black cobbler's wax—heel-ball, Gyp called it—and melted the end of it in the flame. It melted thick and gooey, and he rubbed the gooiness along the edges of the shoe, where the new rubber met the old uppers. When he'd put it there it hardened. He held an old table knife blade into the candle flame, and when it was hot he ran it round the heel-ball and smoothed it nice, like a proper cobbler did.

'That won't let in the wet,' he said approvingly, laying it aside and starting on its mate.

'Shall ah go and tell Noggie ah'm sorry?' I asked him.

He looked at me with surprise.

'You tell Noggie that *you*'m sorry? What in God's name for, lad?'

'For hitting him.'

He was quiet for a bit; and then, when he spoke again, his voice was very firm and very low.

'Nay, chap,' he said, ''Tisn't thee must tell Noggie you'm sorry—it's him who must come to yo' and say *he*'s sorry.'

'So ah were right to hit him, then?'

He finished the second shoe before he spoke again. Then he collected his few tools together carefully and took them into the brew-house, where he kept them. He stood on the doorstep looking at me.

'Understand me,' he said. 'If yo' *hadn't* have hit Noggie for what he said, yo'd never be mate of mine again.'

I saw deep into Gyp's eyes as he said this to me and I knew then that I'd acted true, even if I didn't fully understand the truth of what I'd done. I'd stepped into man's-world for a fraction of time, ahead of my time. . . .

But, even so, I knew I'd got to make it up with my mate Noggie, because neither on us belonged to man's-world yet, and we'd got to keep each other company in a boy's.

'Come inside and have some jam and tea wi' me,' Gyp said, and herded me through the back-kitchen door. His mam was sitting by the hob. Big and happy she was, with half-a-dozen chins to her and a bosom like a boat's life-saver. She wore a man's cap and jacket, and lace-up boots, and she was a happy soul I was always glad to be with.

'He'll have jam and tea with me,' Gyp told her, and her eyes were cornflower blue that twinkled when they looked at you. She took the steaming iron kettle from it's trivet over the fire and poured its water into the waiting pot. Gyp cut thick slices of bread from the unwrapped loaf on the table.

'Dos't want a scrape o' butter on bread?' he asked me. 'It's marge, really, but we calls it butter when we has visitors call.'

'Just on the dry bread,' I answered. 'Butter meks the jam too greasy.'

'Right enough,' Gyp agreed, 'it's same as putting custard on kippers, putting grease under jam. Here bist, then—get stuck in.'

His mam poured the thick brown tea for us, sweetening it and colouring it at the same time with spooned-up gobs of condensed milk.

'How bist yo're mam, then,' Gyp's mother asked me, 'and yo're dad and all?'

'Going along,' I answered, bread and jam cluttering my mouth.

'Ah, then,' she said, 'that's what most folks is doing these days—just going along. That, and no more.'

'Don't get depressing him, our mam,' Gyp told her, 'he's just had a fight wi' his best mate.'

'Can't have that,' she said, 'mates falling out wi' each other.'

'He did right,' Gyp answered, 'and that's the long and short on it. Step down, yes. Back down—no. And he didn't back.'

'Ar, then,' she said.

Gyp finished eating and rolled one of his thin cigarettes. The kitchen of the house him and his mam lived in fascinated me. It was filled with old good stuff, everything with its own story to tell. The thing I liked best was a little square of writing paper stuck inside a frame, like a picture, with glass over it. You could still read the words, although the ink was faded. It was a letter sent by Gyp's great-grandfeyther to his wife—a letter brought back by a crew-member of the ship that had taken the writer to the Australias, a convict ship. The words were all wrong-spelled and clumsy, but they were there for eyes to read and mind to wonder at. It told of the number of prisoners who'd died on the long voyage, and spoke of a hope of being allowed, one day, to come home again. Next to this frame was Gyp's army-buttons and cap-badge, stuck on to leather straps and hung on the wall by his mother, who kept them polished and shiny even while Gyp himself sneered at them. There were sepia-coloured photos everywhere, and pictures cut from books and pasted on to cardboard. There was a rusted sabre and scabbard which Gyp said had been used at Waterloo, and a deer's antlers which Gyp hung his cap and scarf on when he was indoors. There were coloured-glass bottles and paper-weights, a pair of ornamental glass walking-sticks, and glass animals made over a blow-lamp. The rugs round the kitchen floor were made from rabbit-pelts, all cured and scraped by Gyp, and stitched together by him. In a corner of the kitchen was a gramophone cabinet with a big green sound-horn sticking up from it. It was *that* that the Means Test man was telling Gyp's mam to sell when Gyp hit him. Gyp had got some records by a singer called Caruso and Gyp said he was the greatest singer ever, but I knew that Gyp was.

We finished our bread and jam and tea and I walked with Gyp to his garden allotment near the railway-sheds. We trekked through overgrown jungles of wastelands and sprawls of tacky-banks which were slowly covering over with grass and furze, broom and coltsfoot. If I'd been with Noggie we'd have shot our way through, letting off rounds-rapid and lobbing Mills-bombs to get through enemy lines. But when I walked with Gyp, all that seemed kid's stuff.

Quite a few of the out-of-work and the in-work men had their allotments, small patches of ground to till and grow spuds and cabbages in. Some of them were wild-blown and neglected, as if their men had grown tired and dispirited altogether, and even a forwards-looking expectancy of season's food on tables held no attraction for them. Kale and brussels-sprouts' stalks were blowsy with seed, and the weeds as thick as grass. Other men kept their allotments tidy and in wholesome production, and they cursed bitterly when they saw their neighbour's weeds overlapping their own patches, and threatening them with every breeze that could carry seed. Some of the men had built pigeon-lofts and tool-sheds on their allotments, from bits of wood and corrugated-iron sheets scrounged from the tips. The pigeon-lofts were better built than the work-sheds. The lofts were water-tight and smooth finished, so that the birds them-selves would come to no harm. Men who kept pigeons treated them with some deep kindness that was sometimes lacking when they treated their own kids, even. As we passed the pigeon-lofts we could hear the birds roaring inside, a low smooth roar which beat the air like your own fingers feeling the beat of your pulse. Some of the men had opened their lofts and sent their kits of pigeons aloft. They raced round the sky in wide fine circles, following their leader. Over the one loft a tumbler-pigeon did acrobats. Up and down, down and up, like a yo-yo on a string. Couldn't fly a straight line for more than three feet, a tumbler couldn't. You couldn't race 'em. You kept them for their prettiness when they did their acrobatics, for nothing else. Most pigeon-fanciers wouldn't give you half a thank-you for a tumbler. They liked the sleek racers, the homing-pigeons. I stood looking up at the dancing bird.

'It's pretty,' I said.

'The bloke doesn't keep it for its prettiness,' Gyp told me, 'he's got it for purpose.'

'What purpose, then?'

'He's got a new kit of racers. Fetched 'em in a week ago. He put the cock-leader of the kit wi' that hen-tumbler. As long as she stays to the loft, which she will, he'll bring t'others back when it's time.'

It was all so simple it really impressed me.

'That's clever,' I said, 'really clever.'

'Not really clever,' Gyp murmured. 'It's just taking advantage of pigeon-nature. Which is the same as human-nature where cock and cunt is concerned.'

We came to his allotment and I saw that he'd built his pig-sties at the bottom end. Three of them.

'Built 'em while yo' was working in the glass-works,' he said. 'Noggie's dad lent me his hoss and cart to fetch the bricks from where they'd been set in the cut. Now they'm built.'

I looked over the workings, saw how neat he'd laid the bricks and set out the drains, the drains themselves feeding into a cess-pool.

'Where the pigs, then?' I wanted to know.

'In good time. We'll have the pigs.'

'You'n got no money to buy pigs.'

'I's'll have pigs.'

'You need a permit from the Council. Me dad says.'

'I's'll get permit.'

'Dirty things am pigs,' I said, 'dirty smelly things.'

'Meybe. But they smells nice when they bist turned into pork and lying on your Sunday dinner-plate. There's a water-tap over theer by the railway line. I can run a hose-pipe to it for cleaning the sties out. And the muck from the cess-pool can be mixed in with compost to manure the allotments. So there'll be no waste.'

I thought about it.

'What about,' I said, 'when you've got the pigs? What's to stop somebody stealing 'em one night, then?'

'Dogs,' Gyp answered, 'we shall put guard dogs in on running-loops. We shall be four of us in the pig-business, all clubbing together. We's'll have three sows and get 'em fettled by the boar. We's'll raise the young 'uns and sell some of them and eat some of them. If we can do all that, we's'll manage. Ride the hard times out. There's something else. . . .' He led me to the next allotment, taking his spade with him. He scraped with the blade of it for about a foot deep, and I could see rock. 'See that?' he asked me.

'It's rock,' I answered.

'It's coal,' he said. I put my hands down to it and brushed the dirt and dust away. The rock turned shiny-black. Coal it was.

'Can we dig it?' I asked, 'dig it and take it away?'

He shook his head.

'Not officially,' he answered. 'Officially it belongs to the mine gaffers. That mine t'other side of rail-track. This is an off-shoot of their main seam, what we callen a spur. Be rights, it's theirs. They can follow their seam to wherever it leads and tunnel it out. They can rip all these allotments up and take the coal and leave us wi' a tacky-bank of rubble and ashes, if they'n a-mind.'

'You'll lose your pigs, then. They'll dig all up.'

'Not if we keep it quiet and don't tell 'em. Keep it to ourselves. And in the keeping, we can dig a bit of the coal for our own grates. See that hillock?' He pointed to a hill overgrown with bramble and wildness, and I nodded.

'It's my reckoning that's a coal-hill. Tons and tons of it poking up from ground and got itself a skin of grass to hide under. It's my reckoning we can cut that coal, tunnel it out and cart it away. Bit at a time, sithee, just enough to get by on wi'out being greedy.'

'If we cut into the hill, folks will see. The pit-gaffers will see and come and take from us.'

'Not if we'm careful. We'll bell-pit it.'

I'd never heard the word before; the word was a foreigner. I'd heard of deep-pits and open-cast pits, but never bell-pits.

'What's a bell-pit, then?' I asked.

'Romans,' he answered. 'When the Romans touched the fringe of these parts, they bell-pitted. Made small pits to get the coal out—'bout twenty feet deep. Thin at the top, wide at the bottom. Like a pint beer jar stuck upside down. They were easy to work and took little shoring up—the shape of them kept them on the safe side. We could bell-pit that hill, two or three bell-pits, and soon there'd be no hill left. But it would disappear gradually, see—not all of a sudden so's it would be noticed. But gradual, bit at a time. We'd drop it to ground level and let the top-soil cover it, and if anybody *did* suddenly notice that it'd gone, they'd think it was due to underground cave-in.'

I marvelled at the plan.

'Gyp,' I said in admiration, 'you'm going to be a man of means—you'm going to be a gaffer, yet, what with pigs and coal.'

'No,' he said bleakly, 'ah'm going to be *me*. Bloody independent of gaffers, looking after me and mine.'

Inside his allotment shed, stuck to a wall, was an old poster. It was faded and tatty at the edges and corners, but you could still read all the writing.

NOTICE TO COLLIERS

We, the miners employed under Mr. Lloyd intend to drop our tools on Saturday night next August 21st. 1858 and join our friends the miners of West Bromwich, Oldbury, Tipton, on strike, unless our wages be raised from 2/9d to 3/3d. AN APPEAL: We the miners do appeal to the surrounding districts, viz., Darlaston, Wolverhampton, Walsall, who's reckoning is on the above date to adopt the same plan, and follow the same example.

....

'My grand-dad's,' Gyp said. 'My oath, but they had it bloody hard in his day. We'm come a long road since then, even if it still is a hard 'un to tread.' Something was puzzling me, and I asked him about it.

'Gyp,' I asked, 'how much coal do we tekken out of ground, then?'

'How'd you mean?'

'Well, at school, our teacher reckons they dig for coal all over the world. In our country, in Germany, France, America—all over. Ah'm just wondering how much we tekken out the ground, is all.'

'It's a lot,' he said, 'it's a great lot.'

'Hundreds of tons? Thousands?'

'Millions, more like. Umpteen millions.'

'Ar, then,' I said.

He studied me.

'What's on your mind, then?'

'It's saft, really. But this morning ah picked up an apple to eat . . . it looked all solid and eatable. But it weren't so—all the inside was eaten away by grubs. There was hardly anything left inside. Just skin and a bit of apple on the inside. Teach says we tekken oil out of the ground, and coal, and sand and clay and stuff. Seems to me that we bist always taking out and putting nowt back, and we'll end up like the apple, and one day the skin'll give way and we'll fall into the middle and have no where to live.'

His face was thoughtful.

'Ah've never thought of it quite like that,' he said, 'not considered that.'

It pleased me that I'd thought of something he hadn't.

'Bulk,' he said, 'we'm taking bulk away, shifting the balance.'

That was beyond me.

'Sithee,' he said, 'if ah dig a hole in the ground, ah've not interfered with bulk. Ah've wasted nothing. The hole bist theer but so is the dirt ah took from it. But yo' tek a ton of coal from ground and burn it, you'm not left wi' ton of gleads and ashes. You'm left wi' no more than a couple of hundredweight —you'n destroyed eighteen hundredweight of bulk. Now multiply that by millions every day and every year, and ah reckon any bloke wi' ounce of gumption can see trouble up front.' His face was tight and clenched with concentration. But I don't think he followed his thoughts through, like I sometimes didn't in arithmetic class. He seemed to let them go. He rumpled my hair.

'Don't mither,' he said, 'there'll still be enough earth-bulk to measure the size of yo're feet against when yo' grows up.'

7

WE didn't get much coal out of our hill, just one bell-pit's worth was all. The rest of it was bat-coal, hard and grey as slate, unburnable. It acted like a thick skin round a small nut of coal. Gyp said there was probably enough to burn in half-a-dozen different fire-grates for three months, so it was worth fetching out. The men from the allotments took the coal out, four men at a time, working the dusk hours. They cut a ton each time, and Noggie's dad hauled it away with his horse and cart. He got two hundredweight each trip for his trouble. The rest was shared between the men who dug it, each stent of four. Four hundredweight each and two over. The extra two was shared out among two different poor families each trip, the old, sick and many-childrened.

The going-in hole at the top of the hill was a square, no more than four feet each side. Hawthorn trees and furze bushes concealed it to everything but a really close-up look. When the men had dug ten feet down, they started to tun-dish the hole, cut the sides to make them slope away from them. Every so often they'd prop-up with scrounged timber and lobbed tree-posts. It didn't need much propping, really, because the shape of the workings kept it safe enough, and the slate-like bat-coal reinforced it like good pointed house-bricks, so just a prop here and there was good enough. Up to twenty feet down, Gyp let me go down the ladder with him or the men. But after that depth I had to stop topside and be satisfied with peering down on 'em. They'd built a cross-piece of timbers at the mouth, and fixed inside the frame was an old motor-bike wheel with tyre missing. Gyp's farrier mate had made an iron axle for it, with a cog attached to act like a brake when wanted. A rope ran round the wheel rim so that coal-buckets could be drawn up.

'Easiest pit ah've ever worked in,' I heard Gyp grunt. 'It's as easy as picking apples off'n tree.'

'Scrumped apples always taste better than bought ones,' one of his mates answered, 'so ah reckons trespass-coal 'ull burn brighter than that legal come by.'

Gyp told me a lot about coal. Before he told me, I just thought coal was black stuff to burn, nothing more. But he was a living story-book of knowledge; more knowledge he'd got to pass on than any teacher who ever clumped me up the ears for not listening. I think I feasted on Gyp's memories, fittled myself on them like I was ever-hungry.

'It's a pity they didn't figure out the use of coal afore they cut all the trees down,' he said to me. 'Instead of destroying Nature, they could have tekken the groceries already waiting in her pantry.'

'Why'd they cut the trees, then—and who did it?'

'Charcoal burners. For hundreds o' years, they chopped the trees down.'

'Charcoal's for drawing with. There weren't *that* many bloody artists around to use up all the forests you'n told me about.'

'Charcoal was used for smelting iron, you silly bugger. Weren't 'til about seventeen-hundred they found they could use coal instead, after they'd turned the coal into coke by part-burning it.'

As he worked, Gyp painted pictures with words for me to look at.

'It was the Saxons who came to this region and left influence,' he said. 'The warrior-farmers. They killed all the men round abouts, or driv 'em off, and tupped the women. Fettled 'em good. They cleared big areas of forest and planted the land.

98

They took deer from the forests and other game for meat and to mek clothes. Each family staked out its claim, likes settlers of the American West. They built stockades round their clearings to keep out the people they'd driven off. They called their clearings "tons", and that's how yo' gets names like Wolverhampton, Tipton, Bilston, Darlaston and Netherton.'

He paused at what he was saying, and I thought his mind had gone to other things.

'That's why we bist Anglo-Saxons,' I nudged him. 'Ah learned that at school.'

'That's right,' he said. 'In the space of time the Saxons settled every inch of this valley—then the Norsemen come and chucked 'em out. But not for long. The Anglo-Saxons rallied under King Alfred and had a right punch-up. The final battle for the Black Country took place near Wednesfield, and Alfred's men won.'

'You mean *we* won.'

'Ar, then. *We* won. And kept our winnings 'til a new army came to the bloody fore.'

'What army was that, then?'

'Bloody army of gaffers,' he answered darkly, 'bloody army of industrial tycoons and greedy men who can no longer see workmen for what they bist. Only see 'em as tools that help to swell their own purses.'

He felt his words in his mind, ahead of speaking them.

'Sithee,' he said, 'it's not governments and politicians that give a nation its back-bone. The back-bone of a nation doesn't come from its battle-ships and field-guns, its ability to last out longest in barbed-wired trenches. Doesn't come from its battle-fields, sithee. It only spills its blood on battlefields, no matter how much cheering goes into the victory that might follow. The blood of a nation, the backbone, comes from what's gone before. Blue-blood pedigrees don't matter a damn, there's nought to 'em. It's like keeping pedigrees of bee-drones, and holding value to 'em where none is. The blood and backbone of a nation comes from blokes like me and lads like yo', and it was passed into us by our forbears who won out against many

99

odds. We'm soft by comparison. We put up wi' things petty-bloody-dictators and bad government managers throw at us . . . we put up wi' things our forbears wouldn't have tolerated, because they were *men*. Sithee?'

I nodded.

'You'n heard of the doomsday book, at school? Ar, then.'

'Domesday,' I corrected.

'You what?'

'It's Domesday, not Doomsday.'

He chewed this over.

'Ar, then,' he said, 'that's made me happy for the day. Ah wouldn't-a slept all night, not knowing.'

'Go on,' I said, 'go on wi' what you were telling.'

'What's the use? You'm too clever for me.'

'Go on, Gyp,' I pleaded.

'Well, when the King's clerks came to these parts to tek notice of every thing they could put a tax on, they saw that the locals were well bloody fed, sithee. Saw that they were catching the King's deer out'n the forests—although who said it was *his* deer was a bloody liar all round, 'cos fruit of the land belongs to him as picks it. Anyroad, the then-day civil service mind dreamed up a new law. The Lawing of the Dogs it were called. Has't heard on it?'

I shook my head, 'No.'

'Ar, then. Next time yo're teacher starts telling you about the glory of English Kings, *yo'* tell her. The King sent men out wi' hoops, and all the dogs of the district had to be paraded and passed through them hoops. The dogs that went through easy were let go. Them 'uns that were too big to go through were reckoned big enough to pull down the King's deer, so half of one of the dog's front paws was chopped off to cripple it, so's it couldn't do anymore hunting.'

'It were cruel,' I protested. 'It were savage.'

'That's the road it was, anyroad. That's what they did. But the men of this valley were up to it. They just started in and bred smaller dogs, ones that would pass through the hoop and *still* pin a deer. Yo' can trace our modern Stafford bull-terrier back to them beginnings. The country's gaffers created laws that forced men to become lawless so they might live.'

When Gyp went on about the Middle Ages I felt like I was drawn inside a spell; there was something that haunting and lovely about it all. His words were like a paint-brush dipped into many pots of colour, and I *saw* the pictures in front of me, as clear as if they were painted on canvas and I could reach out and touch them.

It seemed to me that time hadn't changed at all, but that every bit of it was part of a long, patterned carpet that kept unrolling. I could *see* the pack-trails and cart-roads which linked village with village, town with town, farm with wood-land. Trails which were the foundations of the English rolling roads of my time, roads which reeled like a man drunk and getting to where he wanted to go only by accident. I could *see* the cultivated settlements, clean-cut in oceans of surrounding woodland and scrub-land. I could *see* the open-field system coming into use, three fields to a set, one being left fallow for each year. All round the clearings the thick dark forests hemmed in, and pockets of moors. Inside the forests were small, shy bands of people called 'delvers' who were the then-day smiths and charcoal-burners. The delvers who hollowed out hills to get coal for domestic fires, as Gyp and the allotment men were doing.

'They never knew, never dreamed, they were the fore-runners of an industry more massive than the world had ever known,' Gyp said, 'them delvers didn't. An industry which would eat up the whole of the Black Country forests like a greedy giant's feast. And, in time, when the trees were no more, men could lift the lid off the earth and fetch the coal out. Black oceans of coal.'

I tried to imagine the black underground oceans, the frozen seas of coal.

'The South Stafford coalfield alone covers an area of ninety square miles, they reckon,' Gyp went on, 'thicker than con-gealed blood in a slaughter-yard. And the Rugely and Stour-bridge seams bist thirty and forty yards, and they doesn't come any better than that. As well as coal there's furnace-clay and iron ores, and stuff, limestone. All the stuff that's needed to mek the world turn faster.'

'How long's the stuff been there, then? Under the ground?'

'Since time began, ah reckons. But up to a couple-a hundred years ago, the mining of it only amounted to back-yeard scratchings. All these ores and minerals were laid in stock afore man strod the earth—formed by England's only volcano, dead afore man was born.'

I could listen to Gyp forever. I could listen to him like I could listen to one of his gramophone-records wi' a good voice singing. Listen to it all through then take the sound-box from the middle of the record and put it on the start again and let it go through the grooves all the way, then do it again and again. Most of his records had a picture of a dog looking into the sounding-horn of a gramophone, and a half circle of writing round the picture said 'HIS MASTER'S VOICE', and that's how I felt, I think. Felt like that dog must've done, warm inside and happy at the voice, even if some of what the voice said was often a bit sad in its telling.

'Dos't know what "fiddling" means?' Gyp asked me.

'Playing a violin,' I answered.

'Not that. Ah means t'other sort. To fiddle—scrounge, cheat, get someat a bit on the dishonest side.'

'Ar, then,' I said, 'like yo' do. And Jacky's dad. And my dad, and the Steersman, and—'

'Alright, shurrup. Yo'n got the idea. Dids't know the expression comes about because of a Black Country bloke?'

'No—tell me.'

'Foley, his name was. One-time Mayor of Dudley. Most of the people in these parts worked at nail-making, but the Swedes invented a quicker and cheaper way of mekking 'em. So Foley went to Swede-land to find out how they did things—he pretended to be a half-wit, sithee, and wandered about over theer playing scrappy tunes on a fiddle. The Swedes took no notice of him, and should've done, 'cos he wormed his way up against trade-secrets and come back with 'em, and was soon beating the Swedes at their own game. From then on, if anybody pulled a sly one, it was called "fiddling".'

Our bell-pit ran out of coal abruptly and finally. We'd only taken a stent of a week's work at it, and it dried up.

'Bloody good job ah didn't sink all me capital into it,' Gyp muttered, 'bloody good job ah didn't goo to the bank and borrow a few thousand, and put thirty or forty men onto it. Ah'd a been bankrupt, now.'

'Why'd it run out?' I wanted to know. 'How can there be a little hill of coal all on its own and all, wi'out it being joined to a seam, then?'

'Coal bisn't like man,' Gyp said, 'with a life-span 'way under the century-mark. Coal bist *millions* of years in the making . . . and more can happen in millions of years than in less than a hundred. If yo' comes into contact wi' one earth-shift, one earthquake, in your lifetime yo'll have had a unique experience. But over millions o' years, the old earth has had shifts and tremors and shakes over every inch of her. It's easy enough to see how a little hillock of coal can get separated from the main seas.'

He'd got a couple of bales of barbed-wire, brought to the bell-pit by Jimmy's dad, and no doubt 'fiddled' from somewhere or other. I held wooden stakes in place while Gyp banged them into the ground with a sled-hammer. We put the stakes three feet apart, all round the mouth of the bell-pit. When they were fixed Gyp took the barbed-wire and stringed it from one post to the next, until the wire was thick-wrapped round as a bush with spikes on it.

'Galvanised barbed-wire,' Gyp said, 'it'll last forever, never rust.'

When we'd finished at the job, we knew that nobody would go falling down the hole we'd dug. Not courting-couples nor kids, nor animals for that matter.

When we'd done we walked away over the pit-fields, as if having been back in contact with coal again Gyp wanted to be among more of it.

The pit-heads were bleak and lonely, yet awesome and exciting at the same time, like a lot of inside-feelings mixed up inside your mind together. The largest pit was building a mountain of tack-bank, cinders and earth and bat-coal all jumbled in together and laid seam upon seam. You got the feeling that the mountain of slag and rubbish was alive and moving, moving at a sly rate that didn't show when you looked at it. But when you looked away and *then* looked back at it, you knew that it had moved forwards a bit. Moved and spread. That's how it looked, and you felt in time the whole mountain would have moved and spread forwards enough to swamp the valley it poised over. On top of the mountain was a narrow-guage rail-track, and waggons of rubbish came away from the pit-workings along these tracks, to be tipped over the edge. The track-waggons, the pit-dobbins, were toy-like all that way up. They looked like match-boxes, and the men working wi' em were little dolls dotting the slag-scape. The pit-wheel in its scaffold of derrick was a big one, towering over its cage-hole, black and creaking. The rope-wires running back to the cage-house hummed with wind and strain. A lot of men worked in this pit. It was one of the few that stayed in full production, and the men worked hard in it so's not to be laid off in favour of somebody else. I tried to imagine them there under the earth, cutting and hauling off, and the pit-ponies pulling the lines of coal-filled carts towards the cage so's it could be winched up. Some pit-ponies were top-side in the colliery fields and getting themselves fettled up on grass and fresh air. They peered at us as if they were nearly blind . . . and Gyp said they were.

'Not so long back, once a pony went down pit,' he told me, 'he never saw daylight again. Worked and fed and slept and died underground.'

'It was bloody cruel,' I said, 'too bloody cruel.'

'It were so,' Gyp agreed, 'and yet even at that the ponies had a better life in the seams than did the people who cut 'em. Kids younger than yo' scratting away down theer, women an' all. Somebody grew fat out'n it all, but it weren't the workers. Things bist better now—there's chain-cutting and engines and the like. And one or two pits have started putting baths at the pit-heads for men to scrub themselves when they come topside. If we can get shot of the slump and work picks up, ah'd say there'd be a steady improvement all round for pit-men.'

'Teacher says we'n got to be proud of our coal-record in the Black Country. She says it was the world's envy.'

That peculiar darkness came across Gyp's brow, like he was angry at something—not at me, but at something he'd been reminded of.

'What yo're teacher means,' he said, 'is what ah'd expect her to mean wi' middle-class outlook. Thinking to the likes of her is as tight as the bloody elastic holding her nickers up.'

'Navy blue wi' lace edges,' I said.

'What bist?'

'Our teacher's nickers. Ah saw 'em once when ah dropped a pencil on the floor, and looked up.'

'That's an experience to last a lifetime,' Gyp muttered, 'that's a sight to mek a man of you.'

The coal-pickers were out at the far end of the big tacky-bank, women and kids with prams and bags picking bits of coal out'n the rubbish.

'Did you ever have an accident when yo' was down pits?' I asked Gyp. 'Were you ever buried under it?'

'Once,' he said, 'ah were once buried under for three days and nights. Roof came down on the gallery we were working in, and five on us got trapped.'

'Were you afraid?'

'My oath, yes. Never more so in all me life. But in a pit-fall you mun never show yo'm afeard, because fear will spread and touch t'others, and if yo' panics and screams and runs about yo'm apt to bring more roof down. Self-discipline is what you have to bring to the fore when you'm caught in a pit-fall.'

I tried to imagine a pit-fall deep underground, tried to see the darkness by shining the light of imagination against it.

'Have lots of pitmen been killed under, Gyp?'

'A goodly number. A lot of men, all over,' he answered, ''specially in the first hundred years of deep-digging. The deep miners had got no experience to steer by, sithee. They had to learn as they went. The methods they used in early times were wonders to marvel at, following on from bell-pit systems. By today's standards they were bloody criminal, primitive-murderous. Everything had to be done by hand, from cutting to hauling off and up to the surface. . . .'

Again I let his words paint the pictures for me, and they were good and easy words, punched out crisp and sharp so that the pictures lost no fine detail. I could see men down in the bowels of the earth, hewing coal and making great clouds of black dust called 'slack', and sometimes when the slack was damp it caused what Gyp said was 'spontaneous-combustion', and great billowing sheets of flame would winnow through the workings, drowning men in the heat of it and scorching them out of existence. Sometimes underground fires started that might take many years to burn out, and the fields and hillsides above the burning would pulse with the heat, and at night time spearpoints of lighted gas would thrust through cracks and crevices.

'Found a chap and a wench dead on one of them fire-hills, once,' Gyp told me, 'they'd come out one night to do a bit o' tupping on the side. Come onto the fire-hill because it was a warm 'un and they got down to business only the gasses got to 'em and they breathed 'em in even while they were rabbiting each other, and it killed 'em.'

He paused, a faint grin hovering round his mouth.

'Strange thing,' he said, 'their moms and dads were naturally upset about their youngsters dying, but they were more ashamed and upset about the fact he was found with his trousers down and her with her nickers down.'

'What sort of gas was it?' I wanted to know, 'that come out'n the coal?'

'There's various gasses in the pits, but in the early days there was more on 'em. Choke-damp was the worst—called "peas-blossoms", on account it smelled like peas-blossoms. Carbonic acid gas was its real name. And there was globe-damp, which was men's breath and candle-smoke congealing into little invisible balloons which floated round the work tunnels. A tallow-dip light stuck on a collier's cap could pierce one of the balloons and set it off like a bloody hand-grenade wi' pin pulled, and it 'ud set off another and then another 'til the whole work-ings blew sky high, and men and hosses wi' it. Bad ventilation was main cause of trouble, as well as bad propping-up. They had to keep small fires burning at the top of the shafts to try and create an up-draught to suck the bad air out.'

I could see it all in my mind's eye. When the underground gases got too bad and pressing for men to work in they were called back to top to sky-side while the fireman blew the gas. He'd light a candle at floor level and tie a long piece of string to it, then get his own arse topside and pull the candle up after him. He'd make the candle swing as he drew it up, 'til the flame went against the gas and exploded it, and cleared it from the workings. When he'd done that, the pitmen would go back down again and take up their stents. They might have to go topside three or four times in one shift.

'The colliers started to take cage-birds down pits with 'em,' Gyp told me, 'canaries, linnets, budgies. At first whiff of gas the birds would topple dead, and give men warning to get from under. It were all as primitive as a Richard the Lion-Heart shit-house on a crusade.'

Why'd they do it, I thought. Why'd men put up wi' it—why didn't they tell the gaffers to go and piddle themselves, and not do it... ?

'Why'd men put up wi' it?' I asked him.

He shrugged. 'Men 'ull put up wi' a lot afore they'll touch breaking point,' he answered. 'They'll let themselves be strod into the ground if they've got families and have to keep the bread on the table. Them early pitmen, they were farmers earlier. But the land got took away from them to be ripped and gutted open for coal and stuff... and they were the ones who had to do it, 'cos there was nowt else for 'em except lie down and bloody starve to death.'

Dark brooding valleys under the earth's skin, dark tunnels wi' ghosts shuffling through them, wicked gobs of coal waiting to drop wi'out creak or warning on to bent backs and gas waiting to blow off like a cooking oven, and sometimes great gushes and rivers of water bursting through as a pitman's iron pierced through to an underground water-swag and let it come through like sea smashing a flood-bank and the men down theer in the big-darkness screaming and blarting and getting tossed about and swirled to deadness, splattered and spun around like when Jimmy and me put little chips of wood into the marley-hole by the skin-works, where the river Stour rushed and screamed and swirled into a big hole. The wood-chips tried to cling to the edges of the hole as if they were alive, but the water sucked and pushed and pulled at 'em 'til they shot under and disappeared. Men like that, under the ground, being buried alive. . . . I felt my mind trembling in its boots, and I wouldn't be a pitman when I left school, not even if they shot me for not being.

'My grandfeyther got caught in a fall at Brierley Hill in the 'sixties,' Gyp said, 'with nine other men and three boys no older than yo' bist. He were down under for four days and nights. The first team of rescuers who went down got trapped themselves, and *they* had to be rescued. They found one of the lad's mam in the cage, trying to get down to the work-level to dig her son out. They found the bottom of the main-shaft was covered wi' twelve feet of water, and they reckoned that nobody down theer could be alive, 'cos the level they were working at was deeper down than the shaft bottom. They put pumps to work and it started to empty at two inches an hour . . . and the crowd on top sent up a big cheer, but then it pissed down wi' rain. Floods thick as thick . . . and water level of pit started to go up. By Saturday the rescue-teams were still trying to get through but were driven back by roof collapses and choke-damp. They reckon that in the four days of rescue they pumped over forty thousand tons of water out of the diggings . . . all they wanted now was to get the thirteen bodies out to give 'em decent burial. For the whole time they worked at the rescue the local chapel and church bells rang out wi'out pause, trying to get Hope through the ground to the pitmen if they be still alive, so's they'd hear the top-noise and take heart. Men pulled the bell-ropes in relays . . . one team tekking ower as another got tired. On the Saturday, the rescue team heard a voice through the coal mass. . . .'

They broke through, Gyp said, but a shift somewhere along the fault sent clouds of choke-damp at them, and they had to pull back for air at the main shaft. They shovelled tons of lime into the workings to try'n kill the gas . . . the rescue-men were stubborn, they wouldn't give up, not while they'd got mates down there. They kept on working, and Gyp's great-grand-dad was among 'em, trying to get *his* son out of the dark hole. And then, Gyp said, on the Monday morning at first light a great ragged thick-deep roar went up from the crowd top-side, a crowd that had been tired and weary and sad up to that moment: 'All saved!'

And they were, Gyp said. All safe. Hungry, thin, two of the lads in coma through fear and hysteria, cold and hunger. But the men with them, by their own courage and steadiness, gave them the will to survive, and live they did.

We went away from the coal-fields and walked the cut-side. I knew Gyp had got his double-barrelled pistol in his pocket and I thought if we got far enough from everywhere he might let me have a shoot. But I didn't want to pester him for a shoot —I knew he'd let me handle the gun when he was ready, in his own good time and not at my insistence. There were narrow-boats riding the cut-waters and I looked to see if I could pick out my Steersman's boat, but he must have been riding another patch. At some of the boat-tillers women sat, with here and there a babby clutched to bosom, wrapped round in a shawl to keep it tied there. Some of the older boat-women smoked clay-pipes, and all the boat-wenches had their hair hanging down their backs in thick rope-like plaits, with a bit of ribbon tied on the ends. The plaits looked like short hoss-reins hanging down. The hooves of the tow-hosses sounded thick and heavy-firm on the pulling-paths, and the sweet musty-nice smell of them came up on the wind. Here and there an engine-boat phut-phutted along, belching muck. My Steersman was right—engines couldn't hold a candle to horses. Horses were best. Up by a lock-gate one horse was rearing up, screeching and snorting and whinnying. Up on his hind legs he went, as if he was going to smash the other horse in front of it.

'He's fighting,' I exclaimed to Gyp. 'He's fighting that other hoss.'

'Not fighting,' Gyp said, 'he's trying to tupp her—he's trying to fettle that mare.'

Boatmen were running along the towpath to pull the stallion off. It reared and plunged, with the mare standing docile, as if nothing untoward were going on.

'The boatman who owns that 'un will get a kick in the arse,' Gyp said, 'letting a stallion draw his boat. Should be gelded—shouldn't let an uncut hoss mix in wi' mares.'

The boatmen couldn't get the stallion away. So they drew back and watched the service. Me and Gyp stood there watching, seeing the big stallion rear up on to the back of the mare. His nostrils were opened and snorting, flared wide, and his grunts and squeals were nearly pig-like. I saw his pole go into the mare, saw her lean back against it to help it. I couldn't move, I was fixed still. The stallion seemed ugly-like, with his back legs holding him up and his front ones wrapped round the mare, and him pushing and heaving and snorting. He looked like elephants I'd seen once at a passing circus, standing on their back legs they were with their fronts resting on the next one in line, and they didn't look right, they looked all wrong. Their front ends seemed suddenly thin and gaunt, as if the weight had drained back into their arse-ends. The stallion looked a bit like the elephants did—all wrong. But he was pushing and heaving and flaring, his pole going in and out, and the mare pushing back on him. I'd never seen the like of it. The boatmen and boat-women stood there staring at the animals, hushed and quiet and watching, and one young boat-wench's eyes were shining as she looked, and her tongue kept wetting her lips. She looked at Gyp a time or two, sly-like, from the edges of her eyes. But Gyp didn't appear to heed her one bit.

'They'm having a good fuck,' Gyp said, more to himself than to me. And *the* word suddenly took on a new meaning for me when he said it. Before, I'd only said it the same as I'd say 'bum' or 'belly-button'. But now, seeing with my own eyes what 'fuck' really was, it burned into me. The word did. It seemed like something you could *see*. It had a sound to it, the word did, that suddenly gave out a dark earth-feeling of magic. Like tree-glooms and damp greenness of ferns and moss, and horse-sweat and man-sweat and mud-suckings and roaring of pigeons and feather-rufflings of birds and thimble-sized field mice. And I think it had a screeching of tom-cats on back-yard walls and the gruntings of bloated bull-frogs and a whirr of grasshoppers in fields of clover. The word suddenly hit me like a warm darkness.

We watched the stallion shudder and finish, and he pulled out'n the mare, and the boat-wenches gave a cheer like crystal-glass shattering ragged, and the boatmen grinned self-con-ciously as if they'd done the tupping in public, and not the bloody hoss. The stallion's pole seemed to shrink away and disappear up inside his belly, like a hydraulic pit-prop wound down.

'What happens now?' I asked Gyp, as the boat-people started to get under way and things settled to normal. 'Is that all there is to it, then?'

'That's only the start on it,' Gyp answered. 'The end of it for the stallion, but the start on it for the mare. Her'll make babbies, now. Her'll have a babby-hoss, meybe twins. In time they'll grow up and pull the narrow-boats.'

That seemed right to me, somehow. This way, there'd al-ways be hosses to pull the boats.

'It's one thing about hosses,' I said with satisfaction, 'they can mek other hosses. But engines can't—engines can't bloody-well tupp each other.'

'No,' Gyp murmured, 'they dussn't know what they bist a-missing, engines don't.'

I thought about things.

'Will ah make babbies, then?' I asked him, 'shall ah be able to make 'em—and when?'

He looked at me side-long.

'Dos't play wi' yo're self?'

I was puzzled.

'No,' I answered, 'Ah mostly play wi' Noggie—we'm mates again.'

'That weren't hardly what ah meant,' he said, 'but it'll do for now. Ar, then yo'll mek babbies when you grow up a bit. It's an easy thing is mekking babbies—yo' don't have to pass a bloody scholarship to be able to do it . . . and if mekking babbies were an industry, there'd be no bloody dole queues, only plenty of overtime.'

8

NOGGIE and me, our quarrel long made up and mended, rode with our Steersman on the Dudley cut. Because he was older than us we called him 'Mister Jobb', and he in turn called us many things besides our forenames. 'Little buggers' and 'young sods' seemed most ready to come to his tongue, but he never said them angry so we knew there was nothing amiss between us. His cabin was a dream, probably better than the hut Robinson Crusoe built for himself on his island. Inside the cabin was a bunk-bed covered up with a patchwork quilt, and all round the walls were horse-brasses nailed on, and an old flint-lock pistol, with bullet-mould and powder-flask alongside. There was a wooden ale-keg in one corner in which he kept a goodly supply of beer to sup when he was moored up overnight between points and not within comfortable walking distance of a cut-side boozer. Inside the cabin he'd got fish-rods and keeper-nets, eel nets and gaffs, the whole trimmings and contranklements of survival. Me and Noggie reckoned that we could ride the boat through the cuts 'til we came to the sea, and then sail out on to the horizons and make our living—a fair living at that—from piracy. Until we suddenly realised that you couldn't get a bloody hoss to walk across the sea and pull the boat.

'Silly bugger,' I said to Noggie, 'yo' should've thought of that—yo'll get us all dronded afore we've got underway.'

'We'll drop this boat, then,' said Noggie, 'and tek over an engine one.'

'Hoss-pulled ones bist better than engine-pushed ones,' I said firmly, 'and that's a Mister Jobb fact which I agree with.'

We were fetching coal from a wharf near the Netherton tunnel, to bring to Brierley Hill, to an iron-foundry there. The Netherton tunnel was a three-miler, three miles long, cutting straight through Dudley hill with its castle on top, to come out on the Birmingham side. It was a grand tunnel, the longest in the country, mayhap the world for all I knew. It was grand enough, but I was glad we weren't going to boat it. When you stood the one end and looked through, you couldn't see daylight at the other. It was just one long ever-stretching tube of darkness, darker than the pits Gyp used to work in.

Some of the tunnels round about had to be legged through. There were no paths for the hosses to walk on, so at the start of these tunnels the horses had to be unhitched and walked round to the other end. There'd be 'leg-men' waiting at each end of the tunnel, men with no regular work to attend. For a little bit of money they'd help the steerer leg his boat through. They all lay down on planks stretched across the boat, and put their feet up against the roof, which was low-hung, and then they'd 'walk'. The boat would push along like that 'til it got to the other end, and the horse could be re-hitched. I went through some of the shorter legging-tunnels: not that I could help to walk the boats; I couldn't, my feet wouldn't reach the roof. Weird in those tunnels, it was. You kept thinking the roof was going to fall down on you, that nothing would keep it away. And you lost all sense of direction; sometimes you got the feeling that the boat wasn't going ahead, that it was going round in circles faster and faster. You had to shut your eyes even in the dark, to get your balance and sense of direction back on an even keel. Bloody weird it was. Or another boat might come up the tunnel towards you, it's front carbide lamp burning a path through the dark. The carbide lamps didn't stretch very far, didn't spread any great comfort of light. The lamp was up front and you were down back, and for all the good the light did to you there it might just as well have been snuffed. Warning lights for dead-ahead was all the purpose they served. But if you were amidship or up front when you saw a bow-light coming up to you, you felt your mouth go dry and your heart beat thick, because you thought the other one was going to slice into you. But never once did we crash. Each steersman kept to his right-hand side of the water-road and gave clearance of a few inches as they passed one another.

'Tunnels have to be kept more dredged than the open stretches,' Mister Jobb told us, 'to keep a good bottom both sides, otherwise one boat might get hisself bogged down in mud and silt. Take some shifting if they bog down inside a tunnel—can't get to 'em to pull 'em off. On straight runs of cut the channel which gives a clear keel is in the middle—the edges am apt to build up and drag a boat, especially if it's got a load in the holds and riding deep.'

'There's nothing to handling barges,' Noggie grumbled. 'After a couple of days at it, ah reckons anybody could do it.'

Mister Jobb pointed the broken stem of his pipe at him.

'In the first place,' he said, 'these'm *boats*, not barges.'

'Same difference,' Noggie insisted.

'Shows how much *yo'* knows about it,' Mister Jobb retorted, 'A *boat* mustn't be more than seven feet across, wide that is, and a barge is twelve feet six across. That's one thing. Moreover, a barge is no longer than fifty feet long and a *boat* bist seventy. A *boat*'s made of wood, like this'n of mine. Barges bist made of iron. There's the differences, young 'un.'

'Ah didn't know,' Noggie said, a bit impressed.

'Yo' knows now,' Mister Jobb told him, 'so let it sink in.'

Noggie let it sink in.

'How fast bist we a-going, Mister Jobb?' he asked, 'thirty miles an hour, then?'

''Bout two-and-a-half,' Mister Jobb answered, 'three miles an hour if the hoss is on the home run and is looking for his straw.'

'That's not fast,' Noggie protested, and I agreed.

'Water's not fast, it's *sure*,' Mister Jobb answered, 'not meant to be fast, it isn't. Allowing for locks, loading and unloading, ah reckon ah travels on average twelve miles a day.'

Noggie and me considered this.

'It's not far,' we agreed between us, 'it's that less-far, it's hardly worth tackling.'

But is *was* worth tackling, and well we knew it. You didn't measure a water-road by the miles put behind you, but by its very nature. Moving or moored-up, it was *boat* and it was *cut* and it was *great*.

Noggie and me locked-through for Mister Jobb, jumped off the boat while it was still under way and raced up to the gates. Together we'd wind the windlass handle which let us move the balance-beam for the gate-paddles to let the water through, roaring and pouring through the sluices to fill the pound or empty it, as we wanted, changing the water level for us to ride on.

But we made the mistake, at first, of trying to open the lock gates by pushing on the balance-beams *before* the water either side had reached the same level. This means that we were trying to push the entire cut back along its own length, mile after slow heavy mile of it. Mister Jobb saw what we were at, and told us to wait pushing until both water levels matched. We found it easy enough after that. All the sweat and graft seemed to disappear out'n the job. It was because water dussn't resist against itself when it's at even level. Mister Jobb said one man standing firm on a quay-side could push a bosting big boat away from him, if he leaned on it long enough—a big ocean-liner. He said it serious, but neither Noggie or me knew if he was serious. He drummed into us not to waste water. He said if we saw another boat coming down-road on the lock, we were to wait for it and pass both boats through together. Seemed a bit daft to us, there was water everywhere, a great road of it, and it didn't seem like any could be wasted. But Mister Jobb said 'don't waste any' so we didn't waste any.

Locking up-hill was a bit easier than locking-down. You just rode the boat inside the lock, the gates being open, closed 'em after you, then opened the other-end sluices. When the boat was riding high, you opened them up easily and out you rode. As we entered the open locks, Mister Jobb half-hitched a rope—which he called a strap—round a bollard anchored in the ground. This kept the boat from banging about as the inrush of water swirled in and set up what he called 'turbulance'... which seemed to Noggie and me greater than a hundred men lined up to piss in a puddle. Sometimes we passed under small bridges which let farmers move their cattle from one field to another, and the bridges had long deep grooves worn into stone-work and iron work through boat tow-ropes being drawn across 'em over many long years. Some bridges had a slit straight through the middle, running in the directions of the canal's flow. It made the bridges seem like they'd been built in two halves—but Mister Jobb said No, they were built that way for the tow-ropes to pass through wi'out untying the hoss.

He'd got a dry touch to his sense of humour, Mister Jobb had, which left Noggie and me doubled up with laughter. It was the way he said 'em. All straight-faced and half-soaked.

When an engine-driven boat passed us, bubbling and snorting and clanking, he looked after it with disgust.

'Sounds like he's got a giggle in his gear-box and a fart-up in his fly-wheel,' he muttered, leaving Noggie and me to add our own touches.

'Got a tizzle in his tiller,' I said.

'Got a bum-hole in his ballast,' said Noggie.

'Got a piddle in his paddle.'

'Got a cock-up in his cabin.'

'Got a ... got a rheumatic in his rudder.'

We were running out of nautical knowledge.

'Got a piss-up in his pudlock,' I said, guessing wildly and blindly.

'Don't talk dirty,' Mister Jobb reproved, 'not 'til yo've left school and can pay yo're own road in life.'

This puzzled me.

'What's *that* got to do wi' it?' I asked.

'Nothing at all,' Mister Jobb replied, 'but it's as good enough reason as ah can think of for the minute.'

When we passed through tunnels of any length, our Steersman covered us all three over with a bit of tarpaulin, like a macintosh. Just to cover our heads and shoulders. Because the roof and curved walls of the tunnels dripped with wetness, steady as rain. Inside the tunnels I saw that Mister Jobb didn't try to steer by the curve of the canal, but by following the curve of the tunnel-roof. He seemed to make the navigation easier this way, and I didn't question it, because he should know. A lot of rubbish got dumped into the cuts, and the rubbish often piled itself up under the bridges and in the tunnels, where the cutting was like-as-not a bit narrower. Old household rubbish, broken pans and old tin cans, or jumbles of other rubbish like zinc and iron sheetings that were no longer wanted by them who'd had them in the first place; bits of furniture, mangles that had given up working, unwanted mattresses. Sometimes a dead dog with a brick tied round its neck, chucked in by some bloody-minded owner who should be barred forever from owning a dog, chucked into the cut to drown because the owner hadn't got a dog licence. Going through one tunnel, our rudder got fouled up with rubbish and Mister Jobb stripped off bare-naked and went over the side and freed it, cussing like somebody who'd decided he didn't want to be a Sunday School teacher.

Noggie and me wanted to go over the side to do it but he said no, that it could be dangerous, and he didn't want our mams and dads round his neck for drowning their poor little sods.

'My dad 'ud probably give you half-a-dollar for doing it,' Noggie told him. 'He says if he'd've had any sense he'd've dronded me at birth.'

'Got more bloody sense to him than I thought,' Mister Jobb replied, going over the side in a big splash. 'Ah bet he felt like cutting his dicky off when he sired yo'.' He spluttered away down there in the tunnel-murky water, then climbed back up and dried himself on a piece of blanket before scrabbling back into his clothes.

We arrived at the coal-wharf and tied up while the loaders filled the hold. Our boat sank deeper into the water under the weight of it, and Noggie and me started to pretend that they were slaves loading bananas and coffee, and bales of stuff, but we got fed up with that game as kid's stuff and let it go. It was depressing, was the coal-wharf. These great mountains of coal stretched all round, and sky-high, so there was nothing but the black to look at. Engines clanked and shunted in the main yard, big as a railway terminus it was, but after a five minutes' watching we'd seen it all. The engines were old and dirty, spewing that much black smoke out'n their stacks you couldn't hardly see what was going on. We were both glad when we'd loaded up, and turned the boat round to get to the iron foundry where we'd got to deliver the load. The hoss seemed not to notice the extra weight he'd got to pull. It seemed not to matter. He took it easy as easy. We passed down one stretch of cut that was being worked on. The banks had been cut back and were being sloped and bricked to stop them ever toppling into the water, and the men working there seemed as high up as a church-steeple, like flies stuck on a wall. I saw they were using the Blue Bricks that Gyp had told me about.

'It's a wonderful bit of engineering,' Mister Jobb said, as we cleared the workings, 'is water-roads. Mile after mile of it, most of it cut with nowt but pick and shovel, brawn and sweat. The rail-roads had it easy—the land had already been surveyed by the cutters, and there was maps for the railmen to go by. But there was bosting battles between the two on 'em afore things settled down, between rail and cut. Both envious of the other, both wanting all the trade.' His eyes seemed to pierce the distance we were heading into, and old memories.

'Afore the railroad came,' he said, 'boating was just another job. Men worked the boats and left their families ashore . . . but when the rail competition started up and undercut prices, the canal-gaffers had to make chops all round. So the boatmen started to tek their families on board their boats to live . . . and to provide a cheap-labour crew.'

With men like Mister Jobb and Gyp you could open their memories like pages of a book, you could peck their words up like they were many-tasting meals. Through them, you could hook-up to the memories their grand-dads handed them and paint the scenes on your mind like you were there at the time.

'Tek Mother Nature and moths,' Mister Jobb said. 'Before

this valley was opened up to coal and iron, when it was all green and country, there wasn't any black or brown moths—they was all white and yellow 'uns. But as everything blackened under smoke and soot, the birds could pick the light-coloured moths out sharp, and gobble 'em up, and the species started to die out in these regions. But Mother Nature stepped in, and almost overnight her changed their colours to dark, so's they'd settle in against the blackness and dirt of everything, and not be noticed.' A mother moorhen with a brood of chicks fanning from her backside cut across our bows and disappeared into the reeds, clucking a gentle cluck as she went.

'Can'st eat them?' Noggie asked, 'are they good enough to eat?'

'Could do,' Mister Jobb replied, 'they taste a bit on the fishy side, is all. Yo' can eat 'em if there was nothing else to put in yo're belly.'

'Ah've never tasted water-birds,' Noggie said, 'not ducks or moorhens or any.'

'A moorhen's not rightly a water-bird,' Mister Jobb told us, 'it hasn't got webbed feet.'

'Ah never noticed that!' exclaimed Noggie, and nor had I. I'd just accepted that they *were* water-birds.

'Could you eat a swan?' I asked.

'Reckon so. If yo' were clammed enough, and had the way of killing the swan. Bloody strong, bist swans. And who wants to kill 'em, anyroad? A right regal bird is a swan, a right treat to look on. Queens and Kings of the water-roads, they bist.'

The cuts had a life of their own, complete and entire. You saw more of it when you rode the water than you did any other way. It was as if you suddenly became part of its life, sort of got into its blood. There were fish, from frying-pan size to jam-jar minnows, or sticklebacks as we called 'em. Beetles and insects, things that swam and things that crawled. But in the country stretches I noticed that a lot of the trees lining the banks were dead 'uns, and I wondered aloud at it.

'Lightening,' Mister Jobb said, 'lightening seems to strike the trees near the water more than anywheers else. Probably because their roots bist more wet with water than most, and they make good electric conductors.' We worked our way through a stair of locks, six of 'em in all, and got on to the home stretch. While we locked through, Mister Jobb put the hoss's nose-bag on so's he could have a snack, then gave him a drink of cut-water from an old tin bucket.

'It was only natural that rail would win over water,' he mused, back at the tiller and the boat underway. 'It had more speed to it. It's a pity that they'm grabbing all there is, though. They should-a shared, not competed. Should-a been brother and sister, not enemies. Even the roses and castles and painted badge-emblems had meaning other than prettiness at one time. Most boatmen couldn't read 'n' write years agone, so they painted their own pictures on the boats to be recognised by. So's each one could be picked out by post-riders or lockhouse-masters who might have messages to pass on, or re-routing directions.'

'It's not finished, is it, Mister Jobb?' Noggie asked, 'not all over and done with, the cuts?'

Mister Jobb looked sombre.

'It's on its last legs,' he admitted, 'nor I doubt it'll ever get back into stride. Boatmen coming home from the war wouldn't come back to water, most on 'em. They'd seen speed and new-ness, and wanted to keep 'em. Not many of us 'uns left, the old brigade. There's probably no more than a hundred of us 'uns left . . . we'n had our innings.'

We left country stretches behind slowly, and came back into the industrial belt. Even the canal water seemed to turn darker, lost its sunshine sparkle. As if it were discouraged and wanted to go to sleep. But I didn't over-dislike the jumble and growl of works and wharf-bays around us, in fact I didn't dislike it at all. It was *different*, but it wasn't a difference I wanted to get away from altogether. It had some attraction that held me firm.

Mister Jobb wouldn't let Noggie and me help him and the foundry men shovel the load out of the boat. He said we weren't big enough yet to handle a number-nine shovel, we'd only get in the way of the men and mayhap do a bit of damage to ourselves. He told us to have a moach round 'til the boat was empty, and then he'd get us home. He pointed to a thicket of bramble growing lush and green at one end of the wharf.

'Blackberries theer,' he said. 'Go and feast yo'selves.'

We ate our fill, topped up a couple of boat-dipper buckets with the black fruits for Mister Jobb's wife to make jam from, then moached round the iron foundry, watching the men at work. The iron-moulders seemed to me slow and deliberate men, cowboy-like with their checked working shirts and sweat rags tied round their throats, trilby hats pushed to the backs of heads like stetsons. Every man wore a thick leather belt low down over his hips, to keep his bladder-muscles firm against the heaviness of his work. The moulders worked wi' black-sand, made from red sand and soot, all mixed up neat and watered to a certain doughiness. The foreman told us not to go into the foundry-shop because we might have or cause an accident, but we could watch through one of the broken windows.

I knew iron-foundries. I often went into the one near our house, to run errands for the workmen, or help them clean up their work-stalls, odds and sods of jobs for the exchange of a ha'penny or even a full penny here and there. As Noggie and me stood at the window looking into the big foundry, I couldn't help noticing that many of the work-stalls were empty. No men working in them. Two places empty for every man working, and them working like the clappers of hell; not swift and flurried work. Slow and deliberate, but steady, like our boat cleaving the water. Getting there, and not piddling at it. The moulders shovelled spades of black sand into moulding boxes, rammed it hard with iron mallets and tools I didn't recognise, then squeezed the whole boxful tight with a hand-lever. As each mould was made, the man carried it away from his bench and laid it on the grey-dusted floor with its mates, line after line of black-sand moulds, to wait for pouring time. When pouring time came, each moulder would have to fetch molten metal from the furnace in a long ladle, and pour his moulds. Hard work, was iron-moulding. No work ever came harder, I don't reckon. Using master-patterns made from brass, each moulder would have to make about forty moulds for his day's stent, depending on what he was making. Might be metal segs, them half-moon's of metal you hammered into the heels and sole-tips of your boots to stop 'em wearing out quick; or it might be radiator keys, like small wheels; or the iron stepping treads you see going down sewers, or halfway up telegraph poles. Other foundries made drain-pipes, castings for motor-cars —and the really big iron-foundries made bosting big things like ships' anchors, and the like. I didn't need Gyp or Mister Jobb to tell me much about iron-works. I'd always known them, ever since I could walk out'n our backyard and on to the street. We lived inside a big circle of iron-foundries, our house did. With glass-works a bit further out, and coal-pits further out still. But I'd always known the iron, smelled its smell, tasted its sulphur in my mouth. Looking into iron-works always made me feel grown-up-depressed, sort of worried, like our mams and dads were worried when there was no money in pockets or purses and the pantry shelf was empty. Worried, because life didn't seem what it should be, natural and good-flowing. That's how the iron-foundries leaned in on my mind, dark and depressing and worrying because I felt once you got in 'em, you'd never get out again, not ever.

Everything in the foundry was grey-dust covered: grey iron, grey tools, dead as a meal without colour to it. The only colour was in the cold congealed slag round the mouth of the furnace, where last-night's waste-pouring had yet to be hacked and chipped away. The slag was like shiny rock, with rainbow colours in it like veins, reds and greens and purples and violets, and shapings of yellowness. Rainbow-colours that you stare at and into, and think you were on Coral Island. Greens and reds and blues and pinks, all veined and jumbled in together like a grabful of coral taken from a story-book tropical sea. But that's all the colour-warmth there was in the place. The rest of it, furnace as well, was grey and bleak and sullen. Gyp had told me that just before he was born a foundry-furnace exploded as the men lined up at it to catch its metal. Some of them cooked where they stood, shrivelled like flies landing on the sun. Others ran away screaming and jumped into the canal to douse their burning bodies, and rescuers who went in after 'em came up sick and gaggling, holding lumps of cooked human flesh which came away in their hands as they took hold.

We heard Mister Jobb calling us across the foundry-yard.

'Bist ready, young 'uns? Ah'm all finished here, if yo' bist.'

We climbed back on to the boat, slipped the mooring ropes arse-end and front, roped the hoss on and got away from there.

'We'm travelling nigh on four miles an hour, now,' Mister Jobb told us. 'The old hoss knows he's heading for his straw.' Sure enough, the big horse was stepping out like he was a racer. Sparks flashed from his huge hooves a time or two as they clattered over a bibble. Over the wish-wash of the cut-water against our knife-front, the hoove-beats sounded thick and heavy as a drum beat.

Nearly home, I saw this little thing struggling in the water. I thought it were a moorhen-chick at first, but when we got closer I could see it was a bird. Mister Jobb saw it as well, and he reached into his cabin for a dipper wi' a long handle on, and he reached out as we passed and scooped the bird in. It lay there gasping and struggling, and we could see all its flight-feathers were matted up with oil. It's long beak kept stabbing at Mister Jobb's fingers as he lifted it out of the dipper.

'It's a kingfisher,' he said, 'a cock 'un.'

'It's got no colours,' I said, 'it's colours bist all faded.'

Mister Jobb stared at it thoughtfully.

'Ar,' he said, 'it lacks colour because it lacks freedom. See how the oil's clogged it up so's it cor't fly anymore. Settled itself to die, it had. And the colours started to drain from it, ah should think. Like a light going out.'

'What'll we do, then? What can we do for it?'

'Clean it,' he replied, 'clean it and let it ride free. In the cabin, on the left-hand shelf yo'll find a small tin of petrol marked 'DANGER' and in the wash-basin yo'll find a lump of soap. Fetch'm here, then.'

I fetched the things he wanted.

'Now a bucket,' he said, and I fetched a bucket.

'Scoop a drop o' water out'n cut,' he directed, 'then tek my knife and shave the soap into it. Keep mixing 'til soap's melted and yo'n got some suds.'

I pared the soap into small flakes over the bucket, while Noggie kept stirring them to melting, and frothing the water into washing-suds. Mister Jobb took up a piece of rag and poured a drop of petrol on to it, then carefully wiped the bird over, keeping clear of its eyes. Gradually we saw the bird-colours come back as the oil was taken away, like as if a dirty window had suddenly been cleaned to let in the outside world. Mister Jobb cleaned thoroughly and carefully, taking all the oil away. When he'd done, he dipped a fresh rag into the soap-suds and sponged the bird all over again, to get rid of the petrol. The bird had stopped fighting and pecking, but his head and long beak turned this and every way, eyes black and beady and again alert.

'Can I hold him?' I asked, and he put the bird into my hands. I could feel its heart beating against my hand like a small regular pump.

'Couldn't ah keep it?' I asked, 'couldn't ah tek it home and put it in a cage and feed it and look after it?'

Mister Jobb was filling his old pipe. He didn't answer me until he'd done, and the pipe was in his mouth and smoking away like a little chimney-stack.

'Do you really want to keep it?'

'Yes.'

'In a cage an' all?'

'Yes—ah'll tek great care of it. Ah'll look after it well.'

'Would you like to live in a cage?'

'How'd you mean, Mister Jobb?'

'Would you, then?'

'No.'

'Ar, then.'

I troubled at it. I wanted the bird, I wanted to keep its colours close by me, make them mine. Mister Jobb was watching me, looking at my face.

'Ar, then,' he repeated.

'No,' I said, 'it wouldn't be fair. It'd be as bad as keeping pit-ponies underground, to live and work and die down there. It'd be cruel to keep it.' I cupped the bird in both hands, with its head pointed skywards, and I bent my knees and then straightened them, with my arms going up, and when I got to my highest reach I opened my hands and let the kingfisher go. It soared up and away, cutting the sky with colours. It dwindled into distance, and for a little moment it reminded me of being a babby, carried down a hillside on Gyp's shoulder with pit-derricks against the sky, and men and boys chasing a little bundle of coloured smoke from bush to bush.

'Will the kingfisher remember us?' I asked Mister Jobb, 'will it remember us for being kind to it?'

Mister Jobb spat a gob over the side of the boat, a brown gob of tobacco juice.

'Kindness doesn't have to be remembered,' he said. 'If it's remembered, it's no longer a kindness—it's a debt.'

I thought on that.

'Ar,' I answered at last, 'that's the way on it, then. Ah'd rather the bird was free to do as he pleases, rather than be tied to me through being beholden.'

'You'm right,' Mister Jobb said. 'That's the way on it, me lover.'

৶ 9 ৫

Gyp's pigs all died. Swine-fever, he said they'd got. Actually, four of them died and the fifth was poorly-bad but still living, and Gyp pole-axed it with a pole of wood, then slit its throat and made it die. Then he took the bodies to the foot of the hill where we dug our bell-pit, poured petrol over 'em, stacked burnable wood and rubbish round them, and set 'em on fire. They burned and sizzled and cooked, and the smell was delicious, mouth-watering, like crisp bacon in a pan.

But the Town Hall inspectors came and looked round the sties at the bottom of the allotment, and took measurements with a big tape marked out in inches and feet, and wrote things in their note-books. Council workers came in a lorry and used hose-pipes connected to cylinders and sprayed the sties and all round them with disinfectant stuff. And a few days later the Town Hall sent police to Gyp and they took him away to the gaol-house for keeping and killing pigs wi'out a permit.

'Ah bloody forgot,' Gyp said to the police, 'honest, ah completely forgot.' When he came up before the magistrates in Brierley Hill court, the bench said Gyp had got to pay a ten-pound fine or go to prison for thirty days. And Gyp hadn't got that sort of money, nor any of his family hadn't. So he went to the gaol-house. I sat on the pavement outside the court-house and blarted—then wiped my eyes because crying wouldn't get Gyp anywhere, and I walked to the farrier to tell him what had happened. First of all I went home and got my money-box out,

127

and there was one shilling and tenpence in it. I put the money in my pocket and went to Cradley, where the farrier was.

He'd got a horse standing, waiting to be shoed, when I got to his forge. Any other time I wouldn't have interrupted, but this was an emergency.

'They'n took Gyp away to the gaol-house,' I blurted. 'The bloody police took him away.'

The farrier straightened himself up from the bending position over a horse-hoof which he was shoeing.

'What happened?' he asked. I told him about the pigs, and the burning of them, and the Town Hall people and the policemen and the magistrates.

'And now Gyp's in the prison,' I said.

He nodded.

'How much was the fine, did you say?'

'Ten pounds—but I got one shilling and tenpence of it. We only need the rest.'

He looked at me, stroking his chin with calloused fingers.

'Ar, then,' he said, 'ah'd best go and get the rest of it.' He went inside his house and came back holding a leather purse.

'How much y'say you'n got towards it?' he asked.

'One-and-ten.'

'That makes it a bit easier,' he said softly, looking at me a bit like a dad or a grand-dad might when he's in sweet temper wi' you. 'Give it here, then.' I counted the coins into his hands.

'I's'll just add the nine pounds eighteen shillings and twopence,' he murmured, 'and we'll go and buy Gyp out'n prison. But ah mun finish this one hoss off, first. Can't let him walk about on three shoes.' He made a five minutes' job of it, and it was finished. The owner led it away, clattering off over the cobbles. The farrier then closed his forge down, collapsing the leather bellows so that no air remained inside them, putting a steel mesh-grid for fire-guard round the still glowing cokes and coals, so that no sudden wind would scamper through the building and scatter 'em. He took his leather apron off, washed his hands and face quickly at the bosh in the yard which also served as drinking trough for horses.

'I's'll just tell missus wheer ah'm going,' he said to me, and walked back into the house. When he emerged he'd got a clean jacket on and a clean neck-scarf, although he'd still got his working trousers and boots on.

'You want to come wi' me to the gaol?' he asked. 'We's'll have to go on the 'bus—it's a fairish ride to Winson Green.'

I didn't want to go. Not to the prison, I didn't. He read it in me.

''S'all right,' he said, 'prison's bisn't places for lads like thee to hang round. They'm second homes to the likes o' Gyp and me, but no need for yo' to be upset by them. They'm hard places, and hopes be that yo'll steer clear on 'em. Leave it with me—I's'll bring Gyp out'n theer. Just pay his fine at the prison-gate, and he'll be let go. Be back this afternoon, young 'un.'

I watched him go. I didn't want to see Gyp in any part of any shadow that hung about a prison. I wanted to see him as I'd always seen him, sure of stride and free, and proudful as he walked. Not like a bird captured in a cage.

Ah'm bloody glad ah didn't keep the kingfisher, I thought, ah'm glad ah let it go. . . .

And another thought struck me. Tomorrow—tomorrow was Gyp's birthday and I couldn't get him a present in because I'd put my one-and-tenpence towards his freedom-money. I'd got nothing to give him, and the thought burned into me. For one-and-tenpence I could have bought him a shaving-brush and a razor, with spare blades, in a little box from Woolworth's, and a hair-comb in it as well. But now I'd got nothing.

I shuffled along, thinking deep, and gradually, bit by bit like sunlight squeezing through a hole in the clouds, an idea started. I quickened up to almost running as the idea got good hold of me. I went to the skin-works near the river Stour and waited for my apple-man to come into the yard, pushing his dobbin. I sat on the wall 'til he came.

'Joe,' I called, 'hey, Joe. . .'

He rested the handles of his dobbin so that the floor took the weight of his salt-load.

'It's yo' then, is it,' he greeted me, 'come for an apple, then?'

129

He put a hand into his pocket, pulled an apple out, dusted it on his sleeve and tossed it to me. I ketched it, smooth as a cricket-ball.

'Thanks,' I said; then—'Joe, there's someat yo' can help me on.'

'What, then?'

'Ah want's someat—come closer, will you, so's ah can say.'

He came closer, stood looking up at me as I sat on the wall.

'What, then?' he repeated.

'I want a piece of leather—a good piece.'

'What'n yo' want leather for? It's not shoe leather we mekken here, it's other sorts of leather. Handbags and suitcase leather, the like.'

'That's the sort ah want. A nice bit.'

'What *for* then?'

'To mekken something out on.'

'What like?'

I thought hard. Gyp's pistol was a secret he didn't want to reach the ears of the police. I couldn't tell on the pistol.

'It's to make a little case with,' I said, 'for a mate of mine— it's his birthday tomorrow, and ah want to give him a present. Ah want to make a little case for him.'

'What's to put in the case?'

'Ah can't say—it's a sort of secret. Just a little case to put something special in.'

He studied me, as if he could read behind my eyes.

'Casn't tell me who the mate bist?'

'My mate Gyp— that's who.'

Light dawned on him without my switching it on.

'Gyp,' he said softly, 'of course—yo'm wanting to make a holster for that shooting-gun of his'n, for that pistol, Ar, then.'

'How'd you know about the gun?' I wanted to know. 'Ah never mentioned he'd got a gun.'

He grinned.

'Goo easy,' he said, 'nobody 'ull ever twit on Gyp, rest yo're mind to it. But Gyp's in the gaol-house up at Brumm. . .?'

'We've raised the money to get'm out. Somebody's gone to buy him out—can I have the leather, then?'

He nodded.

'Ah'll get a piece,' he said. 'Just hold on here a sec.' He went back into the skin-works and was away so long I thought he'd forgotten about me *and* his dobbin standing there. He came back to me with a little bundle, spread it out for me to see.

'It's *yo're* present to Gyp,' he said. 'so you'll not want any interference from me. I's'll just give you a few tips, if yo'd a-mind to listen. Show yo' a few short-cuts.' I nodded acceptance.

'Leather's got a grain, like wood,' he said, 'so cut wi' the grain where yo' can. This piece here is for the gun-case front. This bit's for the back, and this 'uns for the flap. These two bits here bist for the belt to slide through if one's needed. Here's twine to stitch it all together, here's needle for using it with—a saddler's needle, and here's an awl for mekking the holes with. Got it?'

I nodded.

'That's all ah need say, then. Do the best yo' can. Oh, ar— here's some wax for when you'n finished it. Wax the leather to make it soft and waterproof at the same time, sithee. Be rights, yo' should line the case with leather-skin, but yo'll not have time or experience for that. Tek hold, then.' he passed the bundle up to me, and with a muttered but real-meant 'Thanks, Joe' I scooted off home and sat on the brew-house steps to make my present to Gyp.

I took my jack-knife from my pocket and sharpened the cutting edge on me dad's whetting-stone. Then I got a stub of pencil to mark my leather out, drawing on the inside so's not to mark the proper side which would show. It weren't a cowboy holster or a soldier's holster I'd got to make, not a holster for a gun with one barrel and a bulging cylinder. Gyp's gun was slim, with two barrels, slim like a flint-lock one. I'd got to shape it to that. I shut my eyes and concentrated, imagining I was holding the gun again so's I could know its weight and shape and what was needed to hold it snug inside finished

131

leather. I did what the Steersman, Mister Jobb, did when he was painting boat-pictures; I made a picture of the gun come into my mind sharp and clear, and when it was fixed there I made my eyes shine the picture like a magic-lantern on to the leather, and when the picture was there I drew round it wi' my pencil. I cut the pieces carefully, using the knife like Gyp did when he was cutting leather or rubber for shoe-repairs. I cut all the pieces and fitted them together like a jig-saw puzzle. The front and back pieces met flush, too flush—that way, if ah stitched 'em up, there'd be no room to fit the gun in. I took the front piece into the brew-house and soaked it in water, just enough to make it softer. Then I got a round piece of wood and a hammer. I wrapped rags round the head of the hammer to soften its hardness, so's not to put bruises into the leather itself. I laid the piece over the wood, edges curled over, and gently hammered a bit of shape down the middle of it. When I was sure it was worked enough, I took it into our kitchen and dried it in front of the fire. When it was completely dry I saw that there was shape where I wanted it, down the middle of the piece where the gun had to fit. I went back to the step where my tools were and marked with me pencil point where the stitching holes had to be put. Then I made the holes with the awl. It was hard going, and two blisters came up on my fingers, then broke as I worked on. But I got there, bit by bit. I matched the two halves, back and front panels, putting the belt-straps on the back panel first. Then I threaded the saddler's-needle wi' the waxed twine and stitched the two halves together, making sure that the twine was anchored wi' a good knot, and each stitch was regular-spaced. When I'd stitched the two halves together, I put the flap on. There was no way I could fix a press-stud even if I'd got one, so I made the end of the flap round spear-pointed, then crossed a small strap across the front piece of the holster. The flap could now be tucked into it, held firm. The front panel held away from the back one just enough to give a good fit to the pistol. I took the wax that Joe had given me and rubbed it into the leather, all over, as thorough as thorough. It made the leather darker and softer, and I buffed a warm shine-glow into it. I was proud on it— it looked *real* and shop bought. There was bits of leather left over, enough to make a bullet-case to fit on a man's belt. I made it too quickly, didn't plan it enough before starting in. When I'd got it finished it looked clumsy and lop-sided, and marred the holster. I chucked the bullet-bag away, not wanting it to partner the holster. I went back to the farrier's-forge with the holster tied up in a piece of brown paper, and string wrapped round it.

As I went down the cobbled entry to the forge, I felt my heart lift as I heard the rumble of Gyp's voice. He was back. They'd let him out. The farrier's bit of money and my one-and-tenpence had got him set free. I was deep-down glad.

'Hi, Gyp,' I said, him sitting there on the forge step with the old man, both on 'em drinking ale.

'How-do,' Gyp answered, grinning. 'Yo' decided to get me out, then?'

'Wouldn't let it rest,' the farrier said in a mock-grumble, 'kept at me to get the key turned for you. If ah hadn't a-come, he'd a been over there wi' a barrel of gunpowder to blow you out. Meself, ah were all for letting yo' stop theer. Bloody criminal.'

'It's the way ah was brought up,' Gyp answered, 'it's me great-grand-dad's blood in me veins, and his feyther's afore him. Blood will out.'

'Too bloody true it will,' the farrier agreed.

I went to Gyp and gave him the parcel I'd made.

'It was to be yo're birthday present for tomorrow,' I said, 'but ah 'spect it 'ull do as a coming-out'n-prison present as well.'

He took the parcel into his hands, felt it, then undid the string.

'What is it, then?' he asked, puzzled by its shape. He took the leather piece out of the wrappings and held it up.

'It's a gun-case for yo're pistol,' I said, 'a holster to keep it in.' He studied it. Felt it with his fingers.

'Did yo' make this?' he asked.

I nodded, throat-tight.

'Ah thought as much,' he said.

He looked at the farrier as if I weren't there.

'Yo know something,' Gyp said, 'if ah'd searched every gun-smith's in London or Birmingham, ah'd never have come on a betterer holster than this 'un.'

I felt pleased as punch.

'Ah left my gun wi' yo',' Gyp said to the farrier, 'can ah have it back now?' The farrier fetched it, gave it to Gyp's hands. Gyp passed it across to me.

'Fit it,' he said. I checked the gun first, like Gyp told me always to do, to make sure it weren't loaded and primed; never to take anybody's word on it, always to see to it meself every time my hands went to a gun. I put the lovely cool steel into the leather, closed the butt-flap round, pushed the lead-strap through its thong. I gave the holstered gun back to Gyp, and he felt its weight.

'Perfect,' he said. 'It's perfect, me lover.'

He stood up.

'Yo'n earned a shoot,' he told me, 'so come on and let's find a place wheer ah can teach thee. We'll call off at my house for powder and caps, and bullet-balls.'

The farrier was already pumping the bellows of his forge to get the fire to working strength. He'd got work to do, and a long interruption of it to catch up on.

'Ah'm beholden to thee,' Gyp said to him, a bit awkwardly. The farrier shook his head, eyes warm with friendship.

'There's no hurry on it, Gyp,' he said. 'Tek yo're time, don't get nagging yo'self. When work picks up will be time enough, old lad.'

We collected the powder and ammunition and set off for the woods which pointed Shropshire-ways. We set up in a wood-clearing, miles from anywhere. Gyp didn't think we'd be over-looked or overheard by anybody to be frittened of. He set up a target—an old tin-can we'd picked up along the way. Then he showed me how to load. He'd got a glass tube, like half an egg-timer with an open end to it.

'That's the gunpowder measure,' he said. 'Each barrel takes

that much and no more.' He emptied a measure into each barrel, holding the gun so that the muzzles pointed skywards and wouldn't spill their loads. Then he took two of the bullet-balls and entered them at the barrel-ends. They were tight fits and wouldn't go straight down until he poked 'em down with a thin cane-stick.

'Have to be a tight fit,' he explained, 'otherwise they'd drop out when yo' pointed the gun at the ground, and the gas from the explosion would slip past the sides as well. Tight fit means yo' wastes no power, and it also helps the ball to get a spin on by the time it leaves the gun.' He held the pistol by the grip, cocked the two hammers and placed a fulminate cap over each of the two exposed nipples. 'Top-hats' he called the caps.

'That's safety,' he said, pointing to a little lever alongside one of the barrels. 'As long as that's turned to there, it can't fire, not even with hammers back. Allus leave the safety on right up to the second yo' intend to shoot. Never carry a gun, loaded or not, wi' safety off.' I nodded, impatient to get on with it. All this explanation was kid's stuff. Pulling triggers and watching the targets hop was man's stuff. 'Listen well,' Gyp said, a bit sharply, 'ah'm teaching thee. Ah don't waste me time on just anybody, yo' mun understand.'

I paid attention.

'There's a hefty kick to this 'un,' he said, 'heavy recoil. Yo' should be able to manage it. Line the back "V" notch up with the front blade-sight until the top edge of the blade is exact level with the shoulders of the "V". Remember, yo' aim a rifle but you *point* a pistol—as if it's part of yo're hand. Always shoot two handed when yo' can, or rest the barrels on someat. The steadier yo' can make it, the better the shot. Squeeze the trigger, don't snatch or pull. Let one hammer fire, and drop yo're finger to the next trigger for a follow-up-shot if it's needed. Tek a shot, then.'

I lifted the gun in my right hand like he'd shown me, steadied my left hand round my right-wrist, aimed at the can and pulled the first trigger. My hand felt as if it'd been thumped a good clout. I didn't see where the bullet went, 'cos ah'd shut

135

my eyes at the last split second. I took a second sighting and let go with the next barrel. Again, a big thump at my wrist-end where the gun kicked. I saw the bullet squirt a spout of dirt six feet away from the target.

Gyp grunted dissatisfaction, and took the pistol away from me for reloading.

'Pistol shooting teks some getting the hang of,' he said. 'It's not easy like picture-cowboys make it seem like. Takes patience and practice.'

He prised the spent fulminate-caps from their nipples. He blew into both barrels, sniffed at them.

'Take heed of what ah'm saying,' he ordered, 'so's not to have an accident. Muzzle-loading is differenter and danger-ouser than breech-loaders where yo' puts a complete bullet in. Sometime yo' can fire a muzzle-loader, and bits of powder stop in the barrels, smouldering. If yo' pours powder in and there's a spark still inside, it'll have yo're hand off. So always mek sure the barrels bist cool before reloading. Here, then—fill it up.'

I poured the measures of powder in like he'd done, then placed the balls at the mouth-ends and pushed them home slowly and gently with the ram-rod cane. I cocked the ham-mers, checked that the safety was on, then primed the nipples. I pointed the gun at the target and let both shots off in quick timing. I held the butt better, and the recoil-kick wasn't half so bad. As well as that, the two bullets were nearer the target. I loaded up and shot twelve balls, and it was the twelfth one which hit the can and sent it zinging away like a scalded cat.

'That'll do,' Gyp said, 'yo'm getting the feel on it. A bit more work and yo' should make a fair shot. Not too bad for starters.' Gunpowder smoke hung about us like mist. It smelled like fireworks. I liked the smell.

'Gunpowder's not too bad a smell,' Gyp agreed. 'It's the smell of cordite ah can't stand. Reminds me of the bloody trenches.'

Wood pigeons were courting and cooing in the trees now that the shooting was ended. I could see several of them among the branches above us.

'Shall us shoot some, then?' I asked Gyp, 'and tek 'em home and pluck them for supper.'

'Bullet's bist too big,' he answered, 'a ball from this would shred 'em to pieces. Rabbit gun, is this. Best thing for pigeons is a strong air-rifle—good spring-gun. Makes a little enough hole, but yo' can drop a pigeon clean with a head or breast-shot.'

He put the pistol back into its holster, put the other stuff away into his side-pockets.

'You carry the gun,' he said, 'under yo're jersey, in case we'm stopped by erra-body.'

I'd shot the gun.

Gyp was let out of the gaol-house.

I'd given him a present he liked.

I was happy.

'Can I shoot it again sometime?' I asked him as we went from the woods.

'Thee's'll have some more shooting,' he answered absently, eyes scanning around him for tell-tale signs of hares or rabbits, 'until yo' can do it well enough. But yo'd best come by my house one night, and help melt the lead to make some more bullets. The way yo' chucks 'em about, ah shan't have any left.'

We left the quietness of the fields and woods behind us and came back to the closer reality of rows of houses, factory chimneys and foundry stacks cleaving the sky. Back to the ring of horses' hooves on tarmacked roads, the piles of manure with flies feeding from, and the chug-chug of clattering lorries.

10

'It'll be back to school in another ten days,' Noggie said mournfully, 'and we haven't done a bloody thing to brag about. We's'll grow into old bloody men wi'out any memories, except other people's hand-me-downs.'

'What you think we should do, then?' I asked him, 'what ideas you got?'

'What ideas have *you* got?'

'*I* asked first.'

'I asked second. So what.'

'Well,' I said.

'That's it,' he triumphed, 'you'n got no more ideas than ah've got. So stop swanking.'

'I bet you,' I said carefully, not looking at him, 'I bet you what we could do.'

'What, then?'

'We could get up in't night . . . we could get out of our housens, we could meet at the top of our street. . .'

'Then what? Piss up a lamp-post and run away laughing?'

I looked full-square scorn at him.

'We could go over the woods,' I said, 'and we could come back home wi' some rabbits or some pheasants.'

He sat up straight.

'Poaching?' he blared.

'Poaching,' I said.

He started to laugh. Then stopped, like he was standing on one leg inside and trying to catch his balance.

'Could we do it?' he almost whispered, 'really do it?'

'What'n *you* think.'

He thought.

'No,' he said, 'us couldn't.'

'Why not?'

'Well ... because,' he answered vaguely.

'Because what?'

'We'm not up to it.'

'Who says not?'

'What ah mean—we'n got no gear for it.'

I nodded, trying to look wise and knowing.

'My dad's got gear,' I said, 'an so's your'n. They've got purse-nets and they'n got ferrets ... and we can tek yo're dad's dog along wi' us for the walk.'

There was a smiley-look all over Noggie's face.

'It's a good 'un,' he marvelled, 'a good idea—someat to brag on when we go back to school ... someat to mek my dad's eyes pop out when he comes down to break-fuss and sees the bloody table groaning under dozens of rabbits and pheasants. He always says ah'm a bone-idle sod wi' not an ounce of gumption.'

'Mine hardly says *any*thing to me,' I said, 'and that's a bloody-sight worse. Well, then?'

'Yes,' Noggie said, 'my word, but yes. Poaching it is. To-night.'

'Tonight,' I agreed, and we took a blood-brother oath that neither one of us would back down at the last little minute. We both knew if we broke the solemn oath our hair would fall out, and our teeth, and a big lump would come between our shoulder-blades to turn us into hunchbacks. There was one bloke living not far away just like that—bald and toothless and hunch-backed, and nerra Noggie nor me would ever speak to him. We knew from his condition that he'd broke his word to a mate, his oath-word. And the vengeance had struck.

The two on us, Noggie and me, had been with our dads and the men a time or two when they went after rabbits and the like. We'd helped to spade-out the earth-works of a rabbit-bury when the ferrets wouldn't come up, and we'd helped set up the long catching-nets for field-feeding rabbits to be driven into. But we'd never done any of this on our own. There'd always been the men with us to see to things. I knew we could pay ferrets down holes on a line, but I also knew that there was drawbacks to this. If the line entangled with a root under ground, it might mean a deep dig to free it, and I doubted Noggie and me had got the sap to do that. I'd seen it done once, and three strapping blokes were sweating hour after hour to get down to the ferret, digging away with shovels. On the other hand, if we let the ferrets roam free and lost one, there'd be bloody hell to pay with whichever of our dads owned the thing. Sons could leave home forever, but woe betide the son who lost his dad's ferrets.

'We'd best go and talk it over with Gyp,' I said to Noggie, 'just to get a few wrinkles that might help us.'

'He'll tell our dads.'

'Not Gyp won't. He can keep a secret better than a dumb man.'

'A'right, then.'

Gyp scratched his head when we told him what we were about.

'Where you going to work, then?' he wanted to know.

'The big woods, we thought.'

'Not the middle woods?'

'No.'

'That's good. Ah've already got the middle 'uns staked out, and ah'd be obliged if it stopped undisturbed 'til ah was finished. The big woods, yo' say? Why them?'

''Cos I heard you telling the farrier that there's only one keeper up there and that once the pub's bist shut, all he does is go home and to bed.'

'That's good learning,' Gyp approved. 'Always keep yo're ears open for tit-bits like that and you'll not go wrong. What gear yo' tekking?'

Noggie counted them off on his fingers. 'Six purse-nets,' he said, 'dad's pole-cat ferret. A knife apiece, a bull's-eye lantern, box o' matches in case it gets blowed out. Oh, ar—a sack to carry the stuff back home.'

'Dog?'

'Dad's dog.'

Gyp gave it some thought.

'The way ah see it,' he said at last, 'is this. If yo' mangles the nets up, loses or hurts a ferret, gets a keeper's barrel put into the dog or anything like that—you'm for the high-jump when yo're dad ketches you. But if yo' brings all the gear home exact and a bit of fur or feather to show for the night's work, yo're dad mightn't say much but he'll be pleased as punch. Think yo' can do it?'

'Yes,' Noggie said stoutly.

'Yes,' I echoed, voice less definite than Noggie's.

'You've walked the land you'm going to work, ah take it,' Gyp asked, and we shook our heads 'no'.

'Yo' must do,' he advised, 'must always have a plan and always have a map of the place you'm going to work set into yo're mind. First-planning is more important than after-regrets.'

We both felt ashamed.

'Never mind it,' Gyp said, 'we'n all got to learn.' He studied us, thinking.

'Look,' he said, 'ah know yo' wants to do this on yo're own. But it's not always best to work alone. . . . If yo' want to leave it for a day or two, me and some of the blokes bist going out. One night this week. Yo' can come wi' us.'

He must have seen our faces clouding over.

'No,' he said hastily, 'we'll not interfere with yo' two, not at all. We'll work the middle wood while yo' two works the top 'un. We'll be on hand if yo' wants any help, but otherwise we'll leave you be. How's that sound?'

We were silent for a bit.

'We'll think on it,' Noggie said at last, 'and we'll let thee know.'

The same thoughts were at work inside Noggie and me. If we went with Gyp and the men, there'd be no fun in waiting

141

'til all the folks in our housens were fast asleep, and us two creeping out to meet up at the top of the street. We'd not see the family-eyes popping out at the game laying on the kitchen tables when they came downstairs in the morning—three hundred rabbits apiece and twenty-five brace of out-of-season pheasants.

We walked along the street.

'We'd still be working on our own, really,' Noggie said, 'in the top woods. After all, we'n got to be *practical*. It's the pantry we want to fill, really, not our heads wi' bragging.'

The way he said it sounded all grown-up and serious, all responsible. I admired him with a look.

'Ar,' I said, dragging it out so that he'd think *I* was caught up in responsible deep-thinking as well.

'We'll go with the men, and us'll come back wi' the men—but in between we'm on our own.'

'Yes,' I answered, 'on our own. And ah'm a betting yo' that us two will bring more stuff home than all of them put together.'

'Yo' don't have to bloody bet on that,' Noggie said scornfully. 'It's a nose-on certainty that we will.'

All day long we made our preparations. Only once did Noggie yelp an objection, find an obstacle.

'Ah just thought,' he yelped, 'of someat Gyp said—it's not the bloody pheasant-hunting season.'

'So what,' I retorted, 'the bloody pheasants don't know that —nobody's told *them*, ah shouldn't wonder.'

'They won't taste right—they might be poisonous, or something.'

'Closed-seasons don't happen because the game's not fit to eat, Noggie . . . closed-season's to give birds chance to breed, so's they can be thick enough around for the gentry-guns in the Autumn. Gyp says so.'

'Well, if *he* says so,' Noggie accepted, 'there's no gain-saying it.' We carefully got our bits of gear together. A bull's-eye lantern which once belonged to a policeman—a real beauty, it was. You poured lamp-oil into its bottom and lit the small wick just sticking up inside when you opened the hinged front. At the back of the wick was a high-shining steel mirror to reflect all the light frontways. When you closed the front, the light shone through a big glass lens, and the stream of light it cut into the dark was really powerful wi' a hundred-yards' reach to it at least. Strong light, stronger than lorry headlamps. When you turned a piece of the lamp near its air-cowl, a shutter dropped in front of the light to make it dark when you wanted it to be. A little flick, and the light was there again. A real good 'un that would keep your hands warm on a dark night as well. The rest of our own gear didn't amount to much. Noggie had got two old purse-nets, but since he'd used 'em to play basket-ball with, they didn't amount to much. They'd've let elephants through, let alone rabbits. We'd got a knife apiece, but they were a bit blunted up, so we got the whetstone out and keened good edges into the steel, remembering to make good sharp points for belly-slitting what we caught. That was all the tackle we'd got. We'd just have to depend upon the men to lend us what we wanted, and didn't like being beholden to them. We'd like to've done everything for ourselves from start to finish. Noggie eased the way on this.

'Makes no odds,' he said. 'My dad sometimes borrows gear from t'other blokes, and they borrow from him. So we'm acting the same—we'm just borrowing.'

The knowledge was like a smear of ointment on a sore; it eased the irritation.

'Ah knows a chap whose feyther's dead, and left some purse-nets behind,' Noggie said suddenly. 'Ah bet we could swap them from him.'

'What with?'

'Comics and stuff. He never uses the nets—they'll rot afore he uses them. He's not got the gumption to put 'em to use.'

'How many comics?'

''Bout two-dozen should do it.'

'Wheer's he liven?'

'Back of Pensnett—we could walk theer in thirty minutes. Shall us?'

'It's worth a try. Go and get yo're comics, and I'll get mine. See you back here five minutes' sharp.'

We walked Moody's field way, and cut over to Brettel Lane. It was a steep hill. All the houses flanking it seemed like they only wanted the top 'uns given a push, and they'd all come skeetering down like a pack of cards stood on their edges. Tram-lines still glinted in the road, although the trams were long enough done with. Nobody had yet bothered to pull all the tracks out.

Noggie started to laugh half-way up the hill.

'Whass up?'

'Someat ah thought on,' he answered, 'someat me dad told me about.'

'What, then?'

'A bloke he knew—sold this old hoss to another bloke. Told the bloke the hoss was seven years' old. The bloke was going into the scrap-iron business and wanted a good hoss, but knew bugger-all about hosses. So he bought this one off me dad's mate, and he was going up this hill wi' two old brass bed-steads and half-a-dozen tin buckets and ... and ... AND ...' He couldn't get his words out for laughing. He just doubled up and the laugh was like a big string that wouldn't break. I got annoyed with him and thumped him on his back.

'What *happened*?' I demanded. He got his breath back a bit.

'The bloody hoss dropped down dead,' he gasped, 'about here, it was—this spot here. Dropped down dead as a bloody doornail ... and the vet-man came and looked at the dead hoss, and said it died of old age. Said it was twenty-six years' old if it was a bloody day. ....' Laugh-tears started him up again, and I could see the funny side. In my mind's eye I could see the dead hoss, and the bloke who owned it sitting there on the cart wi' his bottom jaw hanging down to his knee-caps in astonishment, and then I was piddling meself with laughing and the more I laughed the more did Noggie. People in the street started laughing as well, although they couldn't know what *we* were laughing on. They all laughed 'cept one old bugger. He threatened to lamp us one wi' his walking-stick; said we were laughing at his gammy-leg. We hadn't until he mentioned it, but we did after. His gammy-leg seemed the funniest thing we'd ever seen, but we had to belt up the hill a fair bit to get away from his stick. I got the stitch in me side and couldn't move, and there was Noggie up front pretending that the old-bugger was catching up on me, and I didn't know whether to piddle meself or run like the clappers, stitch or not. But the old man had gone back into his house, muttering curses like a man-witch. Noggie lay down on his back, legs and arms stuck up towards the sky.

'Ah'm a dead hoss,' he giggled, 'ah'n dropped dead wi' four gammy legs.'

I stood over him with me knife out.

'Ah'm the vet-man,' I said, 'and ah've got to cut yo're throat to make sure you'm proper dead.' he got up from the floor.

'That's not funny,' he said.

It took us an hour to get up to the top of Brettel Lane, a walk which should've lasted no more than fifteen minutes. We dawdled, being in no hurry. And once you got Noggie laughing, there was no stopping of him. He had me doubled up.

'There was another bloke over at Hagley Market,' he said, 'a hoss-dealer. He'd got three hosses up for sale, in a paddock. And this bloke gets interested in 'em, but he only wanted the one. The hoss-dealer kep' telling him how good the hosses on the outside was ... but the bloke war't interested in them two.'

'What bloody *happened*?'

'"For God's sake, gaffer,"' Noggie said, 'the bloke said to the buyer—"Don't tek the middle 'un, the other two 'ull fall down, else."'

I sat on the floor and howled.

'Shurrup,' I snivelled, 'yo'm giving me the belly-ache through loffing.' And this woman going down t'shops saw me lying there, and she stopped by me.

'Yo' all right, son?' she asked me, and I blinked up at her.

'That chap theer just hit me,' I said, and before you could say 'bum' she'd reached out and clouted Noggie a belter round his ears. Noggie's face was a burn of blank astonishment.

'Bloody bully,' the woman said to him. 'Yo' just leave him alone—he's littler than yo'.' She fumbled into her shopping bag and fished out a ha'penny.

'Goo and buy some liquorices,' she said, 'and don't give that sod any.'

When the pain had gone from his head, Noggie saw the funny side. He didn't laugh, but he didn't resent, either. But I 'spect he would have done if we hadn't got some suck out of it.

The back-end of Pensnett wasn't at all good to look at. It was old and musty and there didn't seem much happiness there at all. None of anywhere around was 'posh', but this back-end was real dismal. The houses were all lined up against one another like threadbare tramps huddling up for warmth and to keep each other from toppling over. The houses looked like bricked-up holes to live in, no more. When I'd once walked this road with Gyp, he said the place was a sheer palace to what it used to be, when it was a nail-making centre. I tried to tell Noggie about it like Gyp had told me, but my words didn't have the same colour about them that Gyp's did.

Gyp said there used to be a nasty stench round all these houses, like an invisible shawl lapped around. Smell of urine—piss, he called it—and open sewers, smell of sulphur from the iron nail-making and a thick menace of smoke from the forge-fires. Black smoke always hiding the sun. And he said the whole of the Black Country, once, the whole of the valley from Walsall to Stourbridge was dotted with heapings and clusters of like houses, if they could be called that. All littered with huts and sheds made from bits of wood and iron-sheetings, canvas tatters and bits of brick slapped together wi' mud and nails, slices of turf and pieces of tile and what-nots. And people living in such places: mams and dads and kids and dogs and grand-dads and grand-mams, all mixed in together. And all the sheds and shacks and nail-forge-houses linked together by mud and ooze and dirt and piles of horse-droppings and rutted cart-roads, wi' no real lavatories, not even a shared one between five or six families; stink and smell and tiredness. In some of the houses, up against the roofs—with ropes stuck on to raise and lower as needed—wooden cages like giant bird-cages. At night the baby-children were put into these cages and pulled up to the ceiling out of folk's way, so's they wouldn't be strod underfoot. The dad of the family had to collect lengths of rod from the nail-master or gaffer, haul it home to their cramped back-kitchens or outhouses fitted out with little forges, and make the nails. Everybody from youngest to oldest had to work at it to make a crust.

Kids were now playing in the dingy streets, streets dingier than where Noggie and me lived, which we hadn't thought possible. The entries to the arse-end of the houses looked dark and grim, giving out no welcome. A baby was blarting in an old pram and its mam came out wi' a titty-bag and stuck it into the babby's gob. A titty-bag was a piece of rag with sugar poured inside, then the rag was tied up with string and the sugar-lump stuck into the blarting mouth. The crying stopped, and sticky-sweet guggling sounds came from the pram. We knocked on this one front door, and the boy with the purse-nets stood there in the dark of the passage, jam-stains round his mouth.

'What'n yo' want,' he said to me.

'Noggie wants you,' I answered, stepping back.

Noggie came straight to the point.

'We was just passing,' he said, 'and thought we'd knock.'

'Yo'n knocked, then.'

'Just to say hello, like.'

'Hellow, like.'

We were getting bloody nowhere at full speed.

'Goo on,' I said to Noggie, giving him a nudge.

'Bloody stop pushing,' Noggie told me, 'else ah shall flick you in the lug-holes.' He stood staring at the boy in the door-way.

'We'n got, er—we'n got some comics to swap,' he managed at last.

'Ah bet ah've read 'em,' the boy answered. 'Gis a look.' We

handed the comics to him. He glanced through them, discarding seven as having-been-read.

'What'n yo' want for this lot?' he asked, holding them up.

'We'm looking for nets,' I said. 'Noggie reckoned yo'd got some.'

'What sort-a nets? Fishing nets? Ah'n got none of them.'

'Purse-nets,' Noggie said, 'them that yo're dad used to catch rabbits in. Thought yo' might like to swap 'em for the comics.'

The boy considered.

'The nets bist worth more than the comics,' he decided. 'What else yo' got to chuck in with 'em?'

We fished in our pockets.

'Four alleys,' Noggie said, offering four glass marbles. 'One's a bit cracked.' The boy took them, peered at them, shrugged at them.

'What else?'

We dug deeper into pockets.

'Ten fag-cards,' I said, 'from Woodbines. Pictures of cricketers.' He flipped through the bloody things like he was a card-sharp. He kept three on 'em.

'Ah've got t'others,' he said. 'What else yo' got?'

'These'm bloody expensive nets,' I started to mutter, but Noggie gave me the look to play it quiet and leave things to him.

'Let's see the nets, then,' he said, 'fetch 'em for us to have a look at.' The boy went down his dark smelly passage-way, and we stood in the street waiting for him. Two or three other lads were hanging around looking at us, and I started to get a bit uneasy. If others joined 'em to make a real gang, they'd start on Noggie and me for being strangers and coming into their area. But the boy came back with the nets.

'Best silk-string,' he told us, spreading the nets, 'every knot hand-made. My dad 'ud only have the best.' He was like a bloody door-to-door salesman selling brushes, he was.

'Ar, then,' Noggie said.

'Ar, then,' I echoed.

'Well, then,' said the boy, 'what else?'

'Nothing else,' Noggie told him, 'ah've offered enough as it is.'

'They'm worth a bit, these nets.'

'Yo'd best keep 'em, then.'

I dug a bullet-case out of my pocket, the brass shining where it had rubbed my pocket.

'This bullet belonged to my Uncle Fred,' I said. 'He killed five Germans wi' it—they were standing in a line and he shot and the bullet went through each and every one on 'em and killed 'em stone dead. Uncle Fred got the Victoria Cross for it.'

The boy grabbed the bullet and stared at it.

'Gaw'wwh,' he said, 'is that right? Killed five Germans?'

'My Uncle Bill was wi' his Uncle Fred when he did it,' Noggie said. 'He'd put his word on it as being true.'

The boy stared at the bullet-case. Made up his mind.

'It's a deal,' he said, and gave us the nets. We got away from there quick, before a gang formed to set about us, or somebody came along to tell the chap I hadn't got an Uncle Fred.

Noggie and me spent the rest of the day stealing bits of food from the mams' pantries. Bread and lard, a noggin of cheese, some dried prunes. Then we walked round the market and stole a couple of apples and an orange. We were stocking up wi' food to take on our poaching trip 'cos we didn't know how long we'd be at it, and didn't want to go hungry.

Somehow, two nights later when we did go, we didn't work the top woods as we planned. We worked the middle 'un with the men, four of them in all. Out under the night-sky, it didn't seem so important all of a sudden that we work on our own. The dark seemed big and wide, a lot of it about, so deep you might step off into a big pool of it if you weren't careful. Gyp's mate the farrier was along with us as well. He was a quiet and steady man, his voice never rising above a murmur, low and monotonous so anybody listening a handful of paces away would put the sound of it down to wind soughing in the branches, no more than that. Gyp and the farrier knew the place well. They led us to a hillock which was riddled through with rabbit-holes, and Noggie and me saw that they'd earlier put little twigs sticking up from the ground near each hole.

'There's nine of 'em,' the farrier told us. 'We'n got to account for nine holes, then.' He showed us how to place the purse-nets. We had to drive a peg into the ground at the top of each hole, drive it in a bit on the tight side so's a rabbit couldn't drag it out. Then the purse-nets were placed over the holes, carefully, with a string running from it to the peg. When a rabbit hit the net, it would close round him and the edges of the net would tighten almost like elastic, so's it couldn't get out.

'What about pheasants?' I whispered.

'Talk quiet, don't whisper,' he said back, 'A whisper carries a long way, but a murmur gets lost before it reaches erra-body's ears. No pheasants this trip, chap—we'll leave them 'til later on in the year when they bist fattened up plump and good.'

Once the nets were set, and one hole left open, things seemed to move slow. The dog that Gyp had got with him was quieter than anything I'd ever seen; like a ghost he was, going from one hole to another. He made no sound at all that you could hear, until you got really close to him and you could hear just the heat of his wet breath sliding over his outstretched tongue. He had no time to be petted and fussed. Every time you put your hand out to stroke him, he brushed away. Job-intent only, no time for owt but the job. The men took their ferrets from jacket pockets, two long sleek ones. They held them by the neck-scruffs so's their snake-heads couldn't sink teeth into their hands if they felt a bit on the mean side. They put no collars on the ferrets to put lines on. They were going to let them roam free. But they only put the one ferret down after all. They took the one and rubbed its nose against the backside of the other, then put him to the open hole, holding him there long enough for him to smell the warren-contents down below. We watched his tail disappear down the tunnel.

'Why'd you stick his nose up his mate's bum?' Noggie asked.

The farrier chuckled.

'That's the bloke-'un we sent down,' he explained, 'and this is his missus we'm holding up here. We let him have a smell at her so's she'd stick in his mind and he'd come up easy enough when his work's done. Ferret's bist no different to humans—after a good stent of work, no matter how tired yo' bist, there's nothing better than a good warm tupp.'

It made sense to me, although ah'd never had a good warm tupp.

We seemed to wait for hours for the action. We just squatted round the hillock, waiting for the squeals of the rabbits when they lunged into the purse-nets, trying to get away from the ferret down-under. As soon as they got entangled in the nets, the men would move in and kill them quick. The men were silent, wouldn't even smoke. Wasn't only the glow of the cigarettes which would give them away to patrolling keepers, it was the smoke. It carried on the air a goodly way, and could be smelled. Gyp chewed his tobacco while he waited, like a pit-man at his cutting-face.

I watched Noggie fall asleep. I lay on my back alongside him, looking up at the stars and trying to make my ears listen for the scamper of rabbit-feet under the ground as the ferrets moved 'em. Everything seemed quiet and still ... and when I woke up the dawn was just misting its breath against an edge of sky, and the first birds of morning were chattering and singing.

'Come on, you lazy sods,' the farrier said to us, nudging Noggie awake. 'Let's be getting off home afore the dark's gone and there's people about.'

I sat up, rubbing my eyes.

'What about the rabbits?' I said. He pointed, and I looked where he pointed. Bloody rabbits—three dozen, at least. All dead and quiet and still.

'Wheer'd they come from?' Noggie asked, sitting up in amazement.

'We caught 'em while yo' slept.'

'There's hundreds.'

'Don't brag—there's thirty-two, to be exact.'

'Whyn't yo' wake us to help?'

'We tried to—but yo' didn't want to wake up. We were

going to leave you for the keepers to ketch, but thought better on it.'

All the rabbits had been slit down the middle and cleaned out. The plucks of gut were inside a bag, with stains and blood showing through. The eatable offal was in another bag, ready for sharing out. The men worked fast now that the light threatened. They took their knives and made cuts to the rabbit's back-legs, cutting in between bone and sinews, making a slit. They pushed the opposite leg through the slit, pulled it tight, and it seemed like the two legs were stuck together. They threaded sticks through, so that they could carry a dozen on a stick, all strung along. Me and Noggie carried one stick-full, and the men took the others, the bags of offal and pluck as well. We walked back over the fields and made for the canal. Couple of miles from where we'd ketched the rabbits, by a hedge-side, the men stopped and dug a hole with a spade. They put the gut-rubbish inside the hole and covered it up wi' soil, deep under.

We came to the Stourbridge cut where it passed under the bridge that led to Audnam, and we left the towpath and pushed inside the thickets. We hung the rabbits on to a couple of tree branches spreading five or six feet from the ground, pulled twigs and branches round to hide them hanging there. The farrier took a piece of chalk from his pocket and drew a cross on the trunk of the tree. Back on the tow-path, he stuck a peeled stick into the ground so it pocked up half a foot. On the edge of the cut, on one of the lip-bricks, he put another chalk-mark. If anybody lined up on that chalk-mark and then on to the stick, a straight line onwards would bring them on to the chalk-marked tree where our rabbits hung.

We knew that Mister Jobb would be riding the cut's back soon on a run to the Audnam glass-works, and he'd pick the rabbits up for us and tek 'em back to his place. We'd collect them from there in Noggie's dad's cart, and share them out. The meat would be roasted or stewed, p'raps with suet-dumplings and spuds, and the skins would be dried and salted on the inside for curing, and made into something useful.

My eyes felt that heavy I could hardly keep 'em open. Noggie was in the same state.

'Ah'm tired,' I said, 'ah'm going to bed for a few hours.'

Gyp grinned.

'At least yo've had a night out,' he said. 'At least yo' now know how the bloody food reaches yo're tables and bellies. You'n got someat to brag about when yo' gets back to school—out poaching all night.'

I left Noggie on his doorstep.

'We'n got nothing to brag about,' he yawned, 'ah didn't *see* any of the bloody poaching—ah fell asleep.'

'We were there when it happened,' I answered, 'and we helped set the nets—that must count for something.'

'Ar,' he said indifferently, 'it might count for something—but the only things ah want to count right now bist sheep a-jumping across my pillow.'

11

SATURDAY mornings was made wicked for kids, made wicked
by our women folk. Our mams and grand-mams and older
sisters and the like. Sat'day mornings was when most mam's
stone-coloured their bits of front steps, swilled down the front
fold-yards wi' buckets of water, as if the outside cleanness of
things denied the lack of things inside the houses. Once the
front steps had been stoned and the yards swilled, they'd start
on the kitchen grate, black-leading it to a high polish. Then
big swabs of curtains and beddings and clothes were put to
soak in the iron-hooped dolly-tub out in the back brewhouse, to
wait for Monday morning wash. It was as if the women made
up their minds to make as much misery for the men and lads
as they could, on a Sat'day and Monday. Kitchen floors to be
scrubbed and sanded, rag-rugs taken out into the yard to have
the dust and dirt beat from 'em with a wooden paddle. Folks
who'd only got one set of curtains for the front windows took
'em down for washing, then whitened the windows over with
a sort of chalk-paste which stopped people from looking in to
see what they hadn't got. After the family wash, only the best
things were hung up on the outside lines. Sheets, shirts and
underwear which were darned and patched had to be dried out
of sight of neighbours' eyes. Here and there, some missus might
only have *one* set of bedsheets; they never touched the beds,
only the clothes-lines, washed every week and hung out to dry
to keep up appearances, and only put on the bed if the doctor
had to come. A 'two-sheeter' was what no woman wanted to be

called, but which many a one was: two pairs o' sheets, one to hang out on the line every Monday washday, the other for Uncle at the pawnshop. Pledge them on Tuesday, redeem them the next Monday, still wrapped in the trappings they came in, worth a two-and-sixpenny pledge every week because they'd got lace trimmings like as not—and like as not they were still being paid for at the rate of threepence a week to the tally-man. When they were redeemed the two and sixpence had to be paid to Uncle, plus sixpence interest, so the sheets actually had a turn-over worth two bob a week.

A bloody funny lot, our women. They bred strong and often rapid, but you'd-a thought having babbies was nothing to do with them. They were that secret about what they'd got under their clothes. They were that secret you'd've thought the whole race would've died out through the women not knowing what was what. There was something a bit funny even to us ones, where you'd got women with nine or ten kids pretending they knew nothing about how they got there. Our grannys were the worst. If they saw a wench with open-throated dress or blouse, showing a hint of titty (but never enough to satisfy me and Noggie) they said grimly that the wench was a fast madam and would end up living tally with some feller, which meant bedding with him wi'out a wedding licence.

Puzzled me and Noggie, that did.

'What's with having a wedding licence?' I asked him. 'Ah can understand pig-licences and dog ones, and gun ones. But what's with wedding ones?'

'Dunno,' he answered, as puzzled as me, 'p'raps if yo' does it wi'out a licence, it bosts off in yo're hand, like a gun.'

'What bosts off, then?'

'Ah dunno—someat the wimmen's got but won't let on about. P'raps that's why yo' have to have a licence.'

'Ar,' I said, but not liking the explanation.

'Her's no better than she should be,' our grand-mams would say grimly, 'her's only tuppence in the tanner. Her got put in with the bread and thinks her got pulled out wi' the cakes,' they'd say.

We boys and men hated Sat'days and Mondays. There were to many bloody women bossing us from under feet, and we did our best to get ourselves some place else with a sprinkling of distance between us.

Every Sat'day morning was bad enough, but the ones before going back to school after holidays were worse, because there wasn't much time left, and the women used up what bit there was. So Noggie and me wandered about the place a bit like flags that'd got no poles to wave from. We moached down to the boat-wharf, but Mister Jobb was away on his narrow one for a couple of days, lugging red sand to Kidderminster. Then Noggie's dad came down the road with his hoss and cart and took Noggie away with him. He couldn't take me because there wasn't enough room, what with the load on the cart and the two of 'em. I watched them clip-clop away and felt a bit left out of things, and felt that Noggie was naught but a deserter. I decided not to keep my next apple-core for him, and I wandered off to Gyp's house. He'd got a kit of pigeons from some place, and was rigging up a loft to keep them in. His hammer was knocking bits of timber together as busy as a woodpecker.

'Glad yo've come,' he said, 'yo' can help me knock this pen together.' It was nice to be wanted.

'Hold a brick against wheer ah knocks the nails in,' he directed, 'so's that the ends will bend over and not stick out sharp.' I held the brick against my chest, and the blows of the hammer felt like little bruises coming at me. But the points of the nails bent safely into the wood.

'Where'd they come from, then?' I asked, 'the pigeons?'

Gyp grunted through a mouthful of nails.

'Mate o' mine,' he answered, 'he's gone on the tramp looking for work. He give 'em to me.'

The pigeons roared and cooed from the baskets which held them, waiting for their new home to be built.

'Pigeons bisn't very lovely,' I said, 'not unless they'm plucked and roasted.'

Gyp worked on, banging his hammer, fitting the pieces of wood.

'Wild pigeons bist good for eating,' he answered, 'but tame 'uns bist good for showing and racing. There's nothing finer than a sleek bird.'

'Birds should be free,' I answered, remembering the king-fisher we'd rescued from the cut, and I'd wanted to keep in a cage for meself, 'it's putting 'em in prison, else.'

'These 'uns were born in lofts,' said Gyp. 'If yo' turned these 'uns loose they'd not survive. They'm tame 'uns, not wild.' He seemed to study his words before speaking any more.

'Sithee,' he said, 'men who work under the earth, pitmen and clay-mining men, they've grown up wi' birds, and learned to love 'em. I 'spect it all started with the deep pits, when men went deeper and deeper and come upon gasses. Tekking birds down in the holes with 'em saved many a life—the birds 'ud sniff the first whiff of gas, and topple over and give the men chance to get clear. Men liked to take their own birds down pits, because they knew that their own birds were in top fettle. They could be relied on, see.'

'Did they take *pigeons* down pits, then?'

'Not to warn about gas, no. I 'spect pigeons just naturally came about. Blokes have allus liked pigeons in these parts. A lot of the local pigeons fanciers served as signallers in the trenches, took their own pigeons to war wi' 'em, to be used for carrying messages. And ah know one pitman who'd got a fair distance to travel to the pit he worked at, and he used to take a pigeon down under every shift. When he come back up top he'd let it go, and his missus would see it land on the loft and know it was time to put the kettle on.'

I watched him shave pieces of wood smooth and tidy. He hadn't got a wood-plane; he used a long knife. He gripped the piece of wood by sticking one end against his chest and the other tightly against the wall, then he gripped the knife firmly in both hands, with enough strength to make the blade bend a bit. Then he scraped the cutting-edge against the wood until it came smooth as if sand-papered. He fitted the piece, then started on another.

'How long will they tek to settle in?' I asked. 'Won't they

fly back to wheer yo' got 'em from, when yo' open 'em up?'

'Ah've put the lead-cock in with his hen,' Gyp said. 'Ah shall keep her penned for as long as is needed for him to settle in. He'll not go far from her, and he'll bring t'others back every time.'

'Will you make money, racing 'em?'

'Ah hope so. That's the idea on it.'

We worked almost silently until the loft was finished, and then we took the baskets of pigeons and put the birds into the loft. They fluffed their feathers and roared at the disturbance and strangeness. Gyp took the lead-cock's hen and put her into a separate compartment, where the cock could still see her, but not be with her. Gyp said that if the cock saw too much of her he'd like as not get fed up with her, like any normal bloke.

'Ah need to go into Cradley,' Gyp said, 'to get a couple of door-hinges for the loft-trap. A bloke's promised to mek me a pair.' He put corn and water out for the birds, stood admiring them. He reached in, took one of the birds to show me close up. He spread the wing-feathers, pointing out the spacing of the flight-feathers, the sharpness of the breast-bone and belly-keel which made up a good racer. I could see the oil-sheen of fitness on the feathers.

'These birds only weigh a few ounces apiece,' he told me, 'but they'n got tons o' courage and guts. Once they'm winging for home, no matter how far the distance, they'll keep coming. Nothing'll stop them except death. Birds have been known to come back to their lofts wi' their both feet missing, chopped off against telephone wires . . .'

He put the bird back into the pen, then opened up a bag of fine sand which he sprinkled all over the floor to catch the droppings.

'It's essential the birds bist kept clean,' he said, 'so's they cort catch anything that'll put 'em out of fettle. They tek a bit of looking after, and if yo' bistn't prepared to look after 'em yo've no right to 'em in the first place.'

He closed the pen door and locked it on its temporary hasp,

then sat down against the yard wall to roll a cigarette. I squatted by him, because I knew that when Gyp sat like that, with 'baccy-box on his knee, he was going to tell me things.

'There can be more nobbling of pigeon-races than dog-races,' he said, 'tek my word on it. In dog-racing, the dogs bist always in sight. Not so in pigeon races. Once the birds get skywards, wi' a fair lap of miles in between the sending off post and the home-clock, there's room for the nobblers to start business. Especially on important races.'

'I always thought pigeon-racing was a clean sport,' I queried. 'What sort of dodges do the nobblers get up to, then?'

'Various sorts. Ah'n seen a few. Ah remember Baggy Gordon from the arse-end of Tipton—fair pigeon racer, he was. A good red-chequer he'd got, best racer for miles round.'

He drew on his cigarette and sat silent, letting the smoke blow round his lungs. I knew it was no good pushing him— he'd tell me what there was to tell in his own good time.

'There was a lot of money riding on Baggy's bird,' he said at last, 'his red-chequer was odds-on favourite to win over the other bird. Only two birds in it—Baggy's chequer and another from the loft of a bloke we called "Copper's Delight", on account he wasn't. After a couple of drinks he'd tek on half the bloody police force in a toe-to-toe slug out, and then give 'em first aid while they waited for reinforcements.'

'What happened at the race, then?'

'Ah'm coming to that—don't be so bloody impatient, young 'un. Well, then this "Copper's Delight" feller got some money together and gave it his brothers to lay bets on his own bird at goodish odds. They sprinkled the bets around bit at a time so's nobody would much notice—hast ever been to a pigeon race?'

'No.'

'Ar, then. This is what happens, sithee. At the proper time two judges and a handler comes to yo're loft, and the same number to the lofts of the other blokes who bist racing. Stop watches bist synchro'd all round. The handlers, wi' judges present and watching, teks the birds and puts 'em in the baskets —which has just been checked by the judges to make sure there's no hidden things that oughtn't to be. Then the judges, handlers and pigeons go to the place wheer the birds have got to be let go—there's other ways they do it, but this is the main one. At the exact agreed second, the baskets bist opened and the birds let up. The fust one home is the winner.'

'That seems fair enough,' I said, 'ah can't see owt wrong wi' that.'

'Ar, it *seems* simple enough,' Gyp agreed, 'but not when you'n got blokes like "Copper" around, wi' money riding on the outcome. He knew that racers fly home the shortest distance between two points, and he knows that every second in the air counts. What he did was to have mates set up along the line o' flight wi' lofts of tumbler-pigeons, all female, piddlin' about and showing off right in the line of flight of Baggy's bird. And Baggy's bird was only human. He see'd some nice wenches playing hopscotch in the sky, and slowed down a bit to give 'em the eye. Well, that happened three-four times along the route, and Baggy's bird struck home last and lost the race.'

He stood up, brushed the ash from his trousers.

'Let's go over to the bloke who's giving me the door-hinges,' he said. 'It'll stretch our legs an inch or two.'

'The very worst nobbling ah ever saw,' he told me as we walked along, 'was when a feller shot a winning bird out'n the sky with a twelve-bore shot-gun. He left the district eventually, 'cos nobody ever spoke to him again.'

We walked cut-side way into Cradley, taking our time on it, with the whole day to do the journey in. But even so, no matter how much we dawdled, it was still too quick for me, because nothing could stop the Monday morning clock ticking towards school opening time, and the end of the holiday. Gyp put a hand on my shoulder as we walked along, me scuffing every bibble that came to inside boot-reach.

'School's none to bad,' he said, understanding. 'My oath, I had little enough on it. Wish't ah was in yo're shoes, young 'un. Ah'd stuff my head with learning, and ah'd make someat of meself.'

I let my head grumble down-bent.

'We only learn saftness in school,' I said, pin-stabs of self-pity back of my eye lids, 'only rubbish about kings and queens and stuff.'

'Learn all about 'em as yo' can,' he said softly, 'so's yo' can beware of 'em when yo' grows up. So's yo' can see that it's *them* as is the rubbish, and not the *learning*. Learning's good. Books and writing, and things to do. My oath, but learning's *good.*'

'Ah learn more things from yo', Gyp,' I said, 'ah learn more from yo' and Mister Jobb and Noggie's dad, but more especially from yo'.'

His hand squeezed my shoulder.

'Ah'm pleased yo'm learning from me,' he answered softly, 'as long as you learn only the good things, sithee. Some things needn't be learned, ever. It's the misfortune of some on us to stumble on 'em by accident. I want yo' to grow up straight, see? Into being a *man*, at nobody's beck and call. Nobody's servant. To have pride, to give fair effort for fair exchange, never to be craven. Dos't understand?'

I looked at him, feeling his hand-pressure on my shoulder.

'Ah—ah think so, Gyp.'

'Ar, then. Listen well. Not so many years agone they made blokes like me go into the trenches and fight for what we didn't know about, didn't understand. Don't let the buggers mek yo' do the same. If fight yo' must then fight for what's your'n and what's right—don't fight unless yo' know what it is you'm fighting about and for, and yo' agree with the fighting for it.'

'Will there be another war, then?' I asked thinking of what the grown-ups were saying about places like Abbassyinia and Spain. 'Will there be soldiers marching again?'

He laughed short and sharp, more like a dog-bark than a laugh.

'It'll come,' he said, more as if to himself than to me. 'My oath, but it's coming. Another big-un. And after it's done, there'll be another and another until the one who made us puts his foot out and crushes the bloody lot on us like a lot of nuisance ants.'

'Will you go?' I asked, fear clutching my belly quick and sudden. 'You won't go again, will you.'

I think his hands trembled as he stopped and rolled another cigarette. They seemed to tremble as if a small wind shook at them.

'If ah do fight again,' he said, face bleak and mouth tight as stretched iron, 'ah shall choose the side ah'll fight for. Ah shall make up my own mind on it, and fight for them as ah thinks is in the right.'

It was a small shop we went to, to get the door things for Gyp's pigeon-loft. They were lucky enough to be in work, and their gaffer had got some orders that wanted getting out urgent, and his men were working the whole of the Saturday. They were dripping with sweat as we stood in the doorway looking into the shop; they'd got sweat-shiny muscles as thick as tree-branches. Stripped to the waist they were, except for the sweat-rags tied round their throats. They kept wiping the sweat from their eyes. They'd got these huge hammers which they kept swinging at rods of white-hot metal, so that the sparks jumped and spat back at them and you thought that the hammers and the men would melt. They kept the hammers striking, five men with a hammer each, blow for blow. Shaping the white-hot links into near-circles, leaving enough gap at one end for the next link to be inserted. And when the links were joined into long-enough lengths the open ends were welded shut ... the links looked like big stitches from a giant's knitting-needles. Some of the other men were making springs, and it looked easy enough, but I doubt it was. A man caught up the end of a white-hot bar of steel and dragged it from the furnace with these great iron-tongues, and the end of the iron was clamped on to a machine while another man took up this big long hook and seemed to stroke coils into the metal. When they'd done making it other men mucked in and they picked up the finished eight-foot high spring with their long iron-pincers —like a big glowing snake the spring was—and they chucked it into this bosh of oil where it howled and screamed and spluttered like a ton of spit on a fire-griddle. The men wiped the sweat from them with their rags, and took a rest. They all looked hard and tough as if nothing could ever fritten them. They all knew Gyp, and one of the men went into a corner of the shop and came back with a nice pair of hinges which he gave to Gyp for his pigeon-pen.

'Thanks,' Gyp said, 'much appreciated,' He talked with the men a bit, laughed and joked with them. One of the men was a loud-mouth and started to talk real dirty, but Gyp nodded his head in my direction.

'Yo'n got kids of yo're own, Tummy,' he said, 'yo' should be knowin' better.'

'He talks like that in front of his own kids,' one of the other men said, pulling a face, 'he do' care.'

'*I* care,' Gyp said, looking at Loud Mouth. Loud Mouth shrugged and laughed and walked away.

Gyp wasn't angry—just stern. But he soon forgot about things as he laughed and joked with the men. He kept doubling over with laughter at the word-antics of two of 'em. Deadpan, they were, with never a smile to let on they were joking amongst each other.

'Ah'm telling yo',' the one of 'em said, 'my brother used to work in a tube-works wheer the tubes were so big thet the holes in the middle weighed two ton apiece.'

'That's bugger all,' his mate answered, 'at my cousin's place they couldn't *see* the holes in the middle. At his place, they had to work to thousandths of an inch.'

'How many thousandths bist there in an inch, then?'

'Ah don't rightly know, but ah'm telling yo'—there must be millions.'

Not a smile between them, not a flicker. I could tell from Gyp's eyes that he liked these men, and I wished he'd brought me to see them *before* my school holiday was finished.

He got up, took me by the arm and steered me out'n the shop.

We were crossing the shop-yard and passing between an avenue of piled iron-ingots when we saw Loud Mouth up ahead of us, waiting for us it seemed like. He was lounging against one of the piles, burly-big, and his eyes all squinted up nasty-tempered. He was chewing and I saw his teeth black-stained, and I knew he was chewing tobacco. He spat the quid out as we came up and the blob near enough landed on Gyp's boot. Gyp seemed to stiffen as he walked, and he gently but strongly pushed me to the back of him. Loud Mouth was blocking the path, and made no hint to move. He made me and Gyp stop.

'Shift,' Gyp said, quiet as quiet.

'Shift me, then,' Loud Mouth answered.

Gyp squared his cap on his head.

'Ah'll say once again,' he said, still soft-voiced, 'and no more. Shift out'n the way, Tummy.'

'Try and shift me,' Loud Mouth repeated. And Gyp did. He moved that fast my eyes didn't reckon it. I saw his fist sink deep into Loud Mouth's belly. I saw Loud Mouth's face mottle red and heard the breath whistle out'n him like a bosted balloon; and then Gyp cracked him hard to the jaw with his other fist, and that's all there was to it. Gyp had knocked him out cold, and he lay there fast asleep on his back.

'Never mind him,' Gyp said to me, 'he's less than pig-muck. He'll wake up on his own.'

He didn't seem at all concerned about it, Gyp didn't. It seemed like once the job was done he forgot all about it. He'd just brushed a nuisance out'n the way. I had a deep-down liking for him as big as a gasometer, and wished he was my dad forever and ever, and I could grow up and do things that would make him proud of me forever and ever. And I wished Monday morning would never come but that I could always be free to go with Gyp and the farrier, and Mister Jobb, but Gyp especially. . . .

'School,' I said, with sinking heart, 'it's back to school on Monday.'

'Never mind it,' Gyp said, with a piece of smile of sympathy, 'school 'ull soon pass—and the day will dawn when yo'll regret its passing.'

'It's a waste-a time!' I raged. 'School's a waste-a time. It—it

164

gets in the way of *useful* things, like cuts and boats and pigeons and shooting. *Them*'s the real things o' life.'

He looked steadily at me.

'Ah'll not gainsay them things bist real enough in their way, chap,' he said, 'but they bisn't all there is to life. Go to school and learn—learn how to put the world to rights that we 'uns buggered up for you. There's no jobs for the likes of me—but there is for the likes of yo', if yo'll knuckle down to it.'

I sat with him for a long time at his pigeon loft while he let the blue-chequer cock circle the air high above, leading the kit, carving shapes from the wind. The shapes were as graceful as a glass-cutter's hands, and the sunlight combing through the oil-sleek feathers put me in mind of the rainbow colours shining out from the furnace slag-heaps after they'd grown cold. But more than anything, I think the blue-chequer bird cutting through sky reminded me of Gyp . . . up front of the rest, leading, making his own time and his own pace.

It was growing towards dark and Gyp rattled the corn-tin to call the birds down. Their circles grew tighter and tighter, but none would drop before the blue-chequer leader. He took his time a bit, then came down fast, drawing the others with him as if they were tied to his backside by string. One by one they entered the loft through its little trap-door. Gyp shut them up for the night before turning to me. He stood easy and kind, looking down at me.

'Has't had a good holiday, then?'

'Oh—yes!'

'Enjoyed theeself?'

'Best time ever.'

'Ar, then. Get to bed early tonight and tomorrow, chap. Get fresh for school so's yo' can learn. Ah'll bid yo' goodnight for now.'

He went inside his back-kitchen and closed the door. I felt lonely because I'd wanted him to ask me inside to share cocoa wi' him and his mam by their ash-grid, and when he shut the door behind him I felt like he'd shut me out'n his life and gone away forever. . . .

❧ Epilogue ❧

Towards the end of the filming I found myself standing in a small street of still intact pre-war back-to-back houses. There in the cobbled fold-yard there was a time-slip, and I was a child again, with hollowness inside me as I watch Gyp go into his back-kitchen and shut the door behind him, as final as a closed book. . . .

Upstairs I stare out through the broken panes of a bedroom window, looking out on part of the Black Country valley, listening to ghosts whispering from the walls. And it's childhood memories I find riding the surface of my mind, not green salad-day memories, all of them. Some are dry and musty as old bran . . . but some are fresh as a new-peeled stick, blooms of clover in fields thick with weeds. I can see little glimpses of the past: a chimney-stack here, an old street lamp there, a bit of corrugated iron on an old shed roof, a kit of pigeons flying round an old man's loft . . . punctuation marks from chapters of the past.